Elementary Music Theory

San Marco Publications

Mark Sarnecki

Book 3

Elementary Music Theory © 2023 by Mark Sarnecki. All rights reserved.

All right reserved. No part of this book may be reproduced in any form or by electronic or mechanical means including Information storage and retrieval systems without permission in writing from the author.

ISNB: 1-896499-02-4

Contents

The Orchestra	3
Ledger Lines	4
The Woodwind Section	7
Key Signature Review	8
Scales Ascending and Descending	10
Minor Scales	13
The String Section	22
Half Steps and Accidentals	23
Review Quiz 1	28
Major and Perfect Intervals	31
The Brass Section	37
Time Signature Review	38
Dotted Quarter Notes	39
Sixteen Notes	41
Triplets	44
Dotted Eighth Notes	45
The Upbeat	47
Rests	48
Review Quiz 2	51
The Percussion Section	55
Triads	56
Review Quiz 3	64
Music Analysis	68

The Orchestra

An orchestra is a large group of musicians who play together using different instruments.

The orchestra is divided into groups of instruments called sections. The four sections of the orchestra are:

>strings
>woodwinds
>brass
>percussion

The orchestra is led by the conductor.

The following picture shows where all the instruments are placed when the orchestra plays.

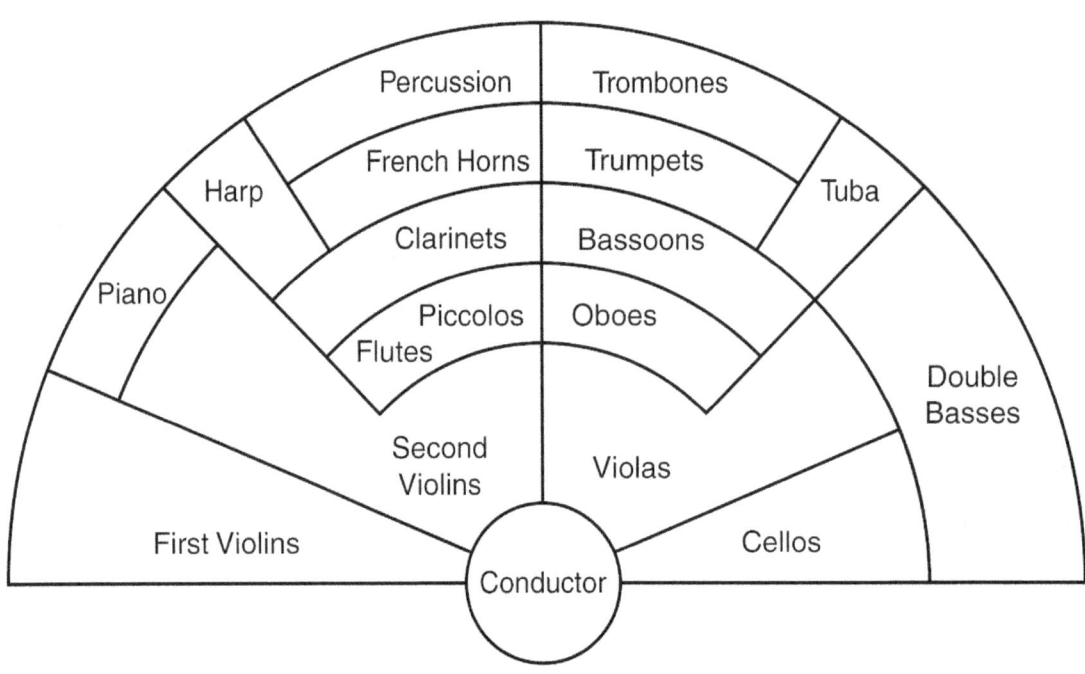

Ledger Lines

We use small lines called ledger lines to extend the range of the staff. These lines are used for notes that are above or below the treble and bass staves. Middle C is on a ledger line.

Here are some notes on ledger lines above and below the treble staff.

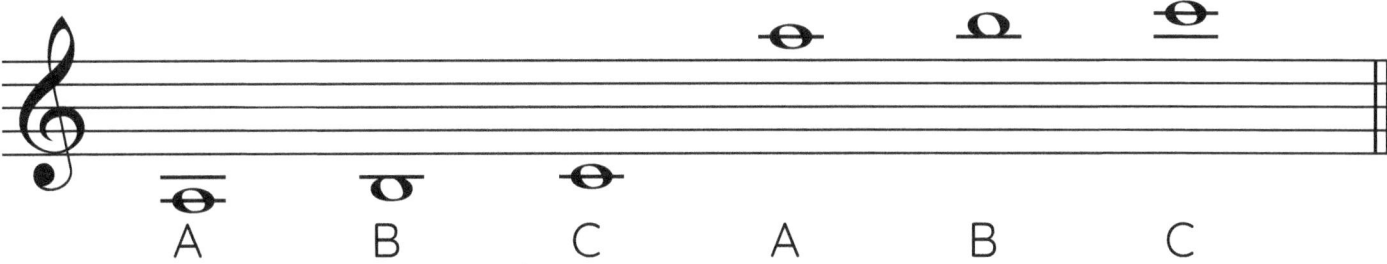

Here are some notes on ledger lines above and below the bass staff.

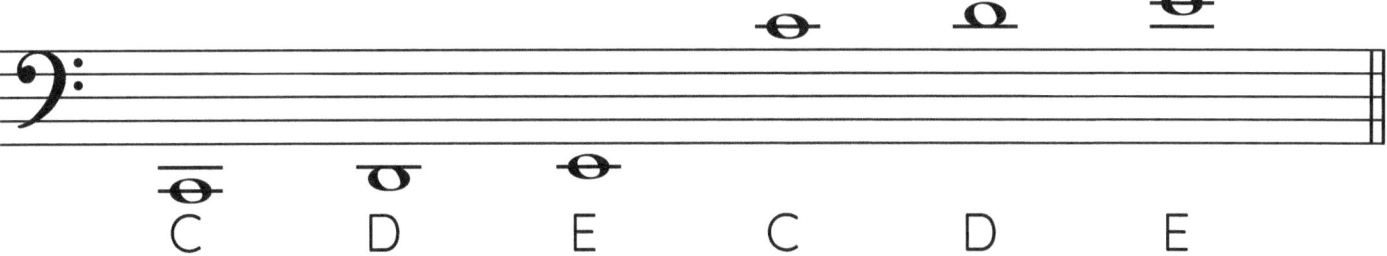

When drawing ledger line notes, always space the ledger lines the same distance apart as the lines of the staff.

1. Name the following notes.

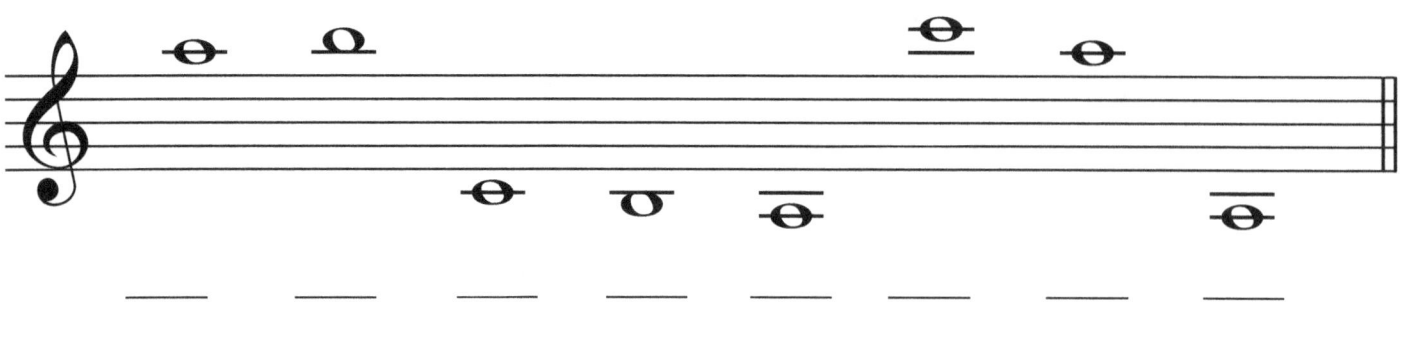

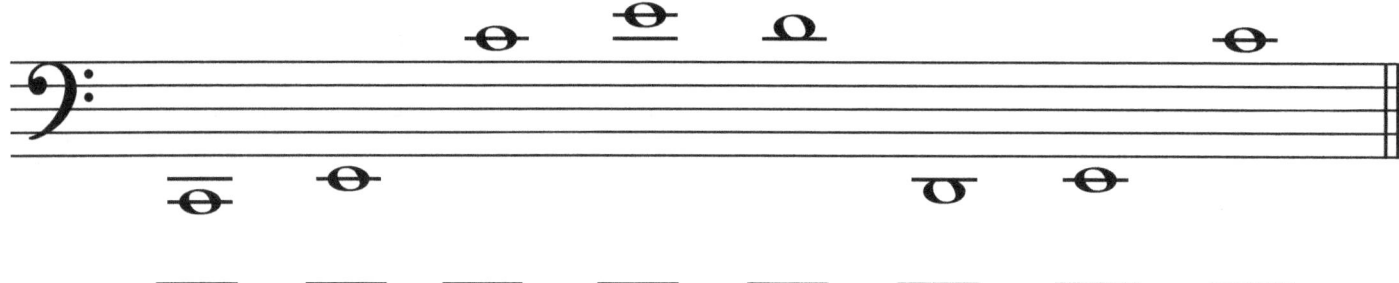

2. Write the following notes using ledger lines above and below the staves. Make sure no two notes are the same.

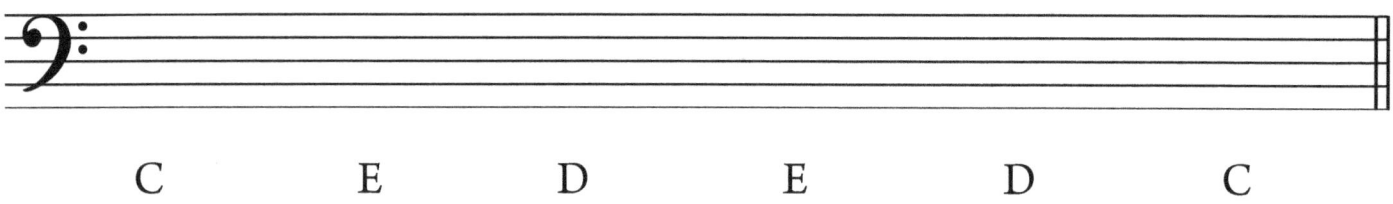

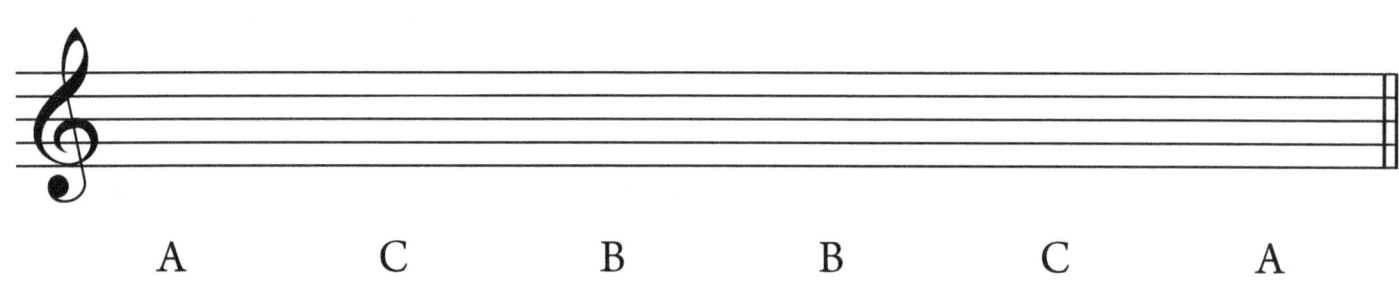

3. Name the following notes.

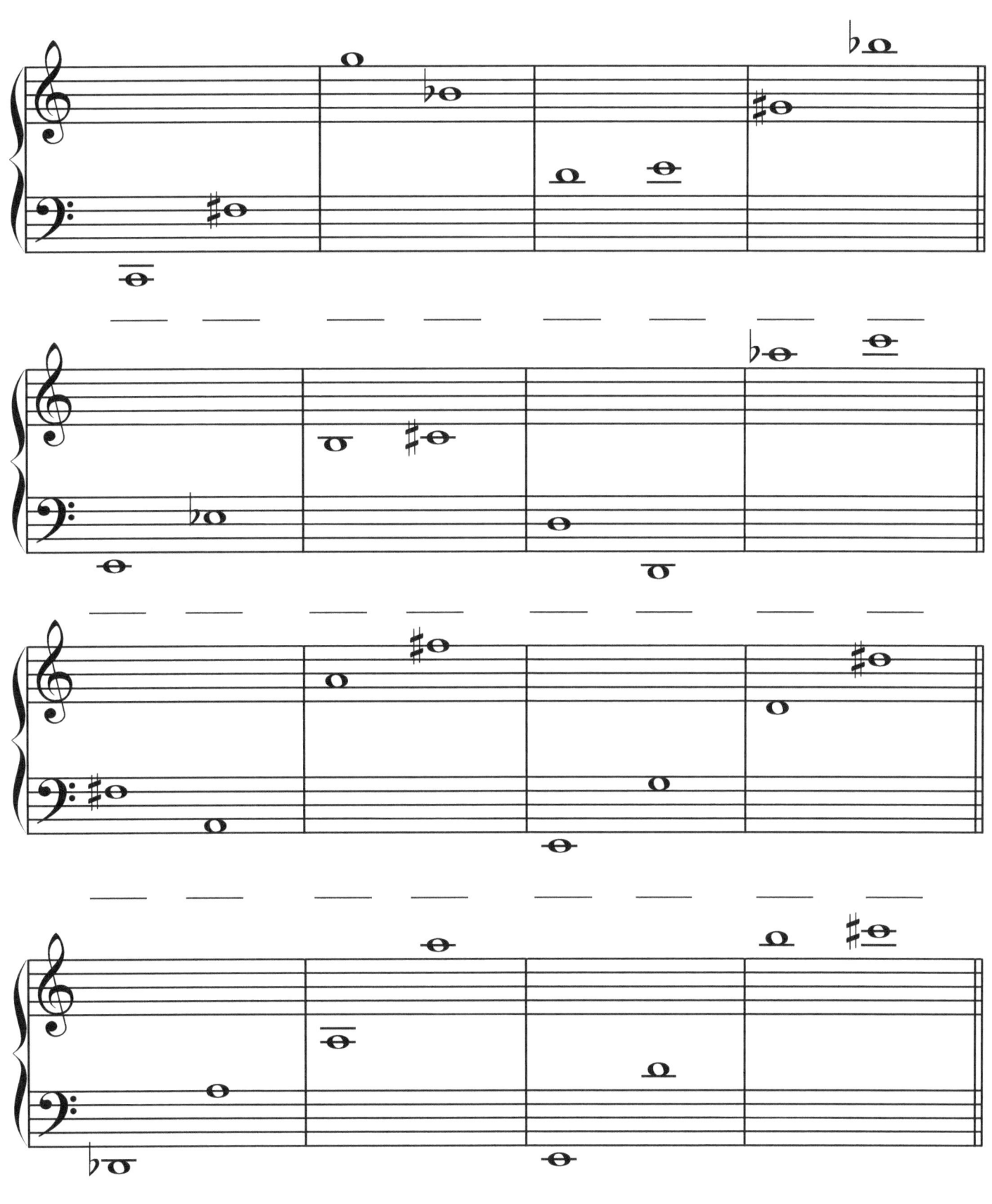

The Woodwind Section

Woodwind instruments are played by blowing into or across the mouthpiece. Some woodwinds use a wooden reed on the mouthpiece. To change pitches, the player uses their fingers to cover holes and/or press keys.

Members of the woodwind family include:

piccolo
flute
clarinet
oboe
saxophone
bassoon

Key Signature Review

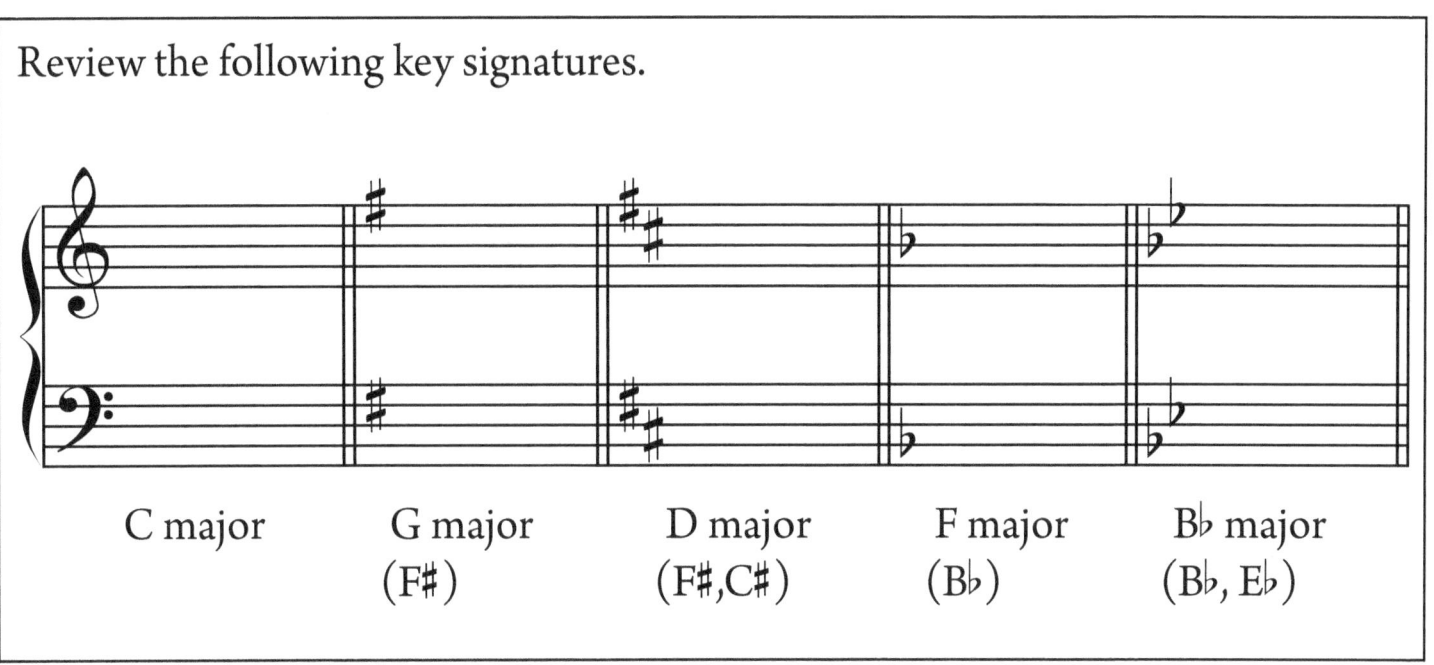

Review the following key signatures.

C major   G major (F♯)   D major (F♯,C♯)   F major (B♭)   B♭ major (B♭, E♭)

1. Write the following scales ascending using key signatures. Make sure the flats and sharps in the key signature are in the correct order and are on the right lines and in the right space.

D major

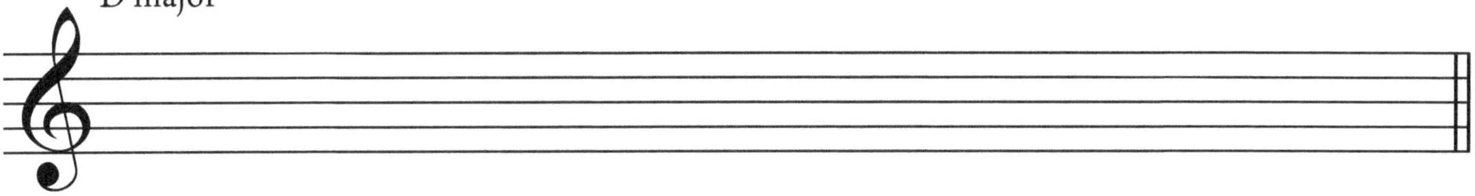

F major

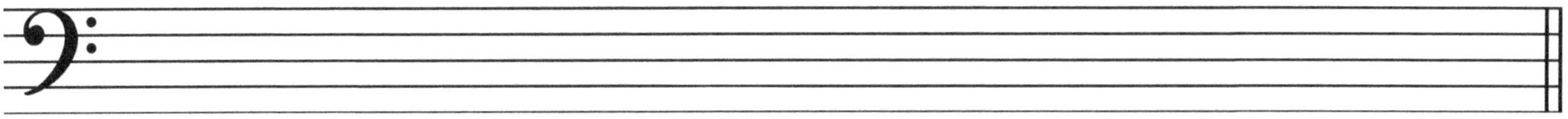

G major

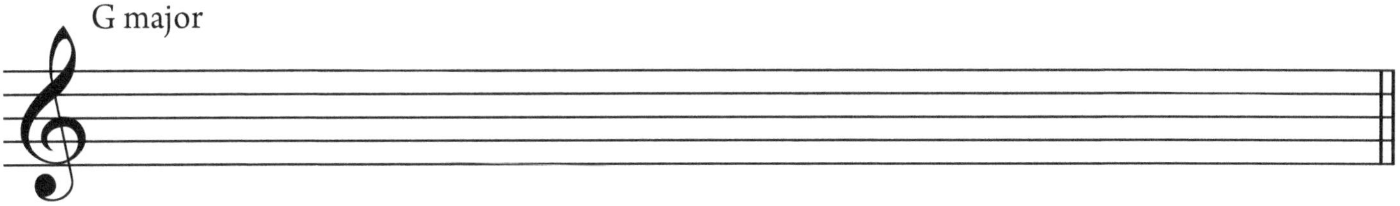

B♭ major

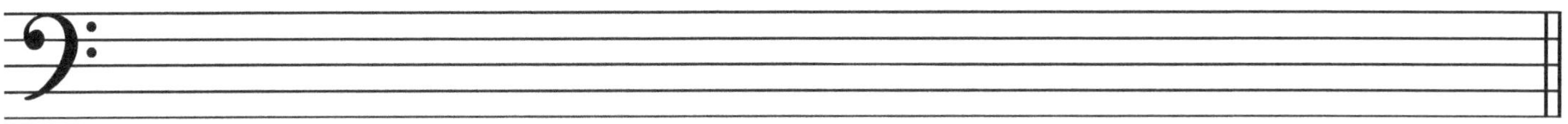

2. Write the following key signatures on the grand staves below.

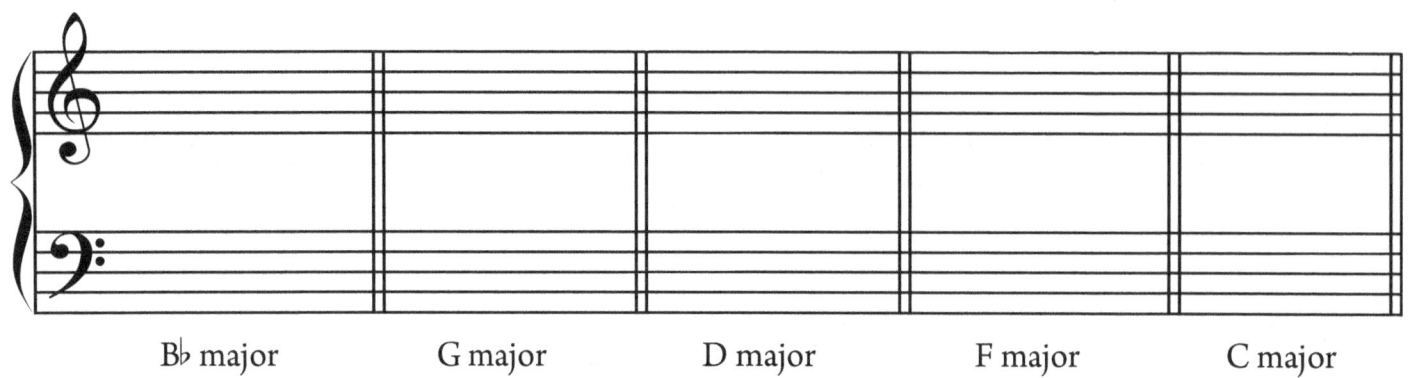

Bb major   G major   D major   F major   C major

3. Add clefs and key signature to form the following scales.

D major

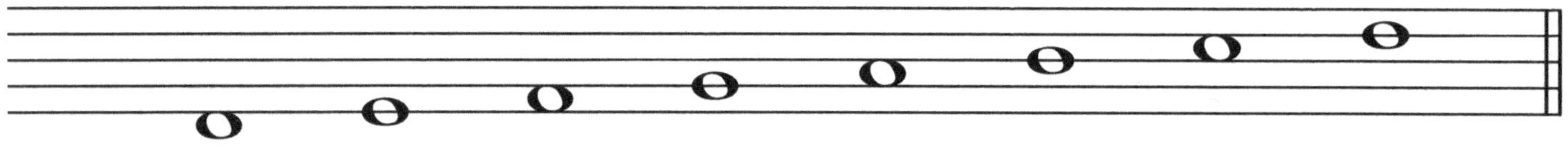

C major

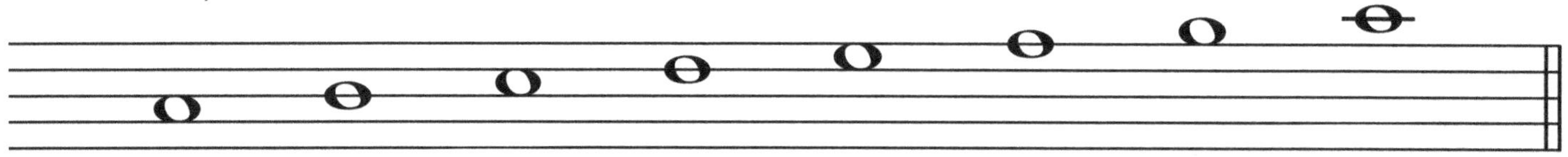

G major

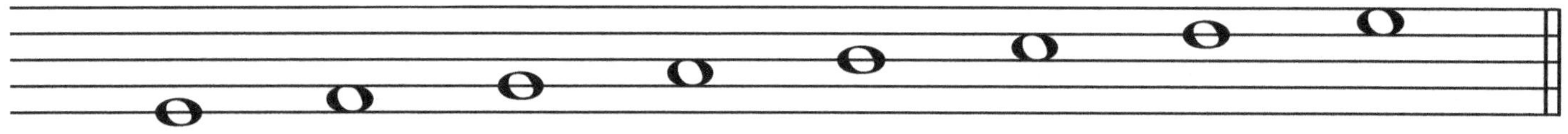

F major

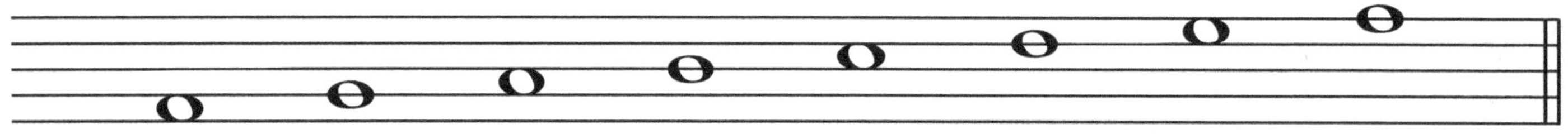

Bb major

Scales Ascending and Descending

When we play scales on our instruments, we usually play them going up and down. Until now we have only written scales going up (ascending). We can also write them going down (descending).

Look at the following example of the G major scale written ascending and descending using a key signature. Remember that when you use a key signature you do not have to write any accidentals in front of the notes.

The first note of any scale or key is called the tonic. This is the most important note in any key. The tonic of C major is C, The tonic of B♭ major is B♭, etc.

The second most important note of any key or scale is the fifth note. The fifth note is called the dominant. The dominant of C major is G, which is the fifth note of the C scale (C D E F G).

For the following G major scale, the tonic is G and the dominant is D. The Gs have been labeled with a T for tonic and the Ds have been labeled with a D for dominant.

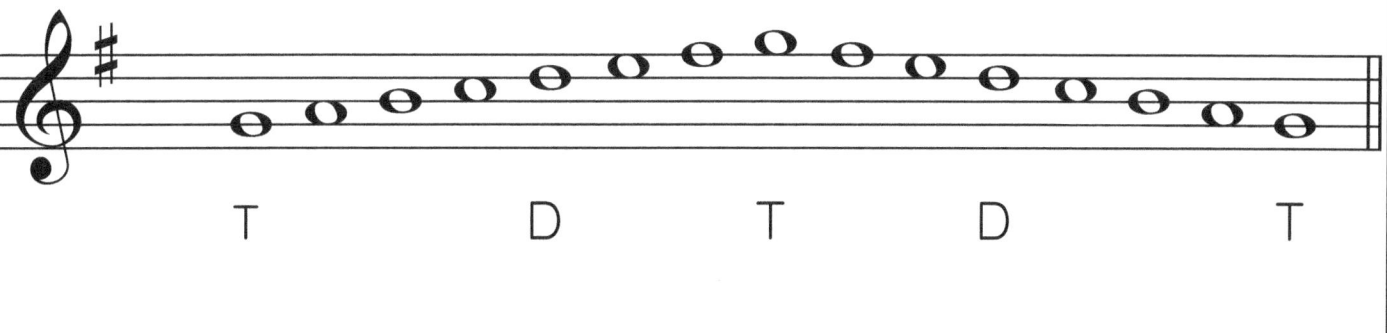

1. Write the following scales ascending and descending using a key signature. Mark the tonic (T) and dominant (D) notes on each scale.

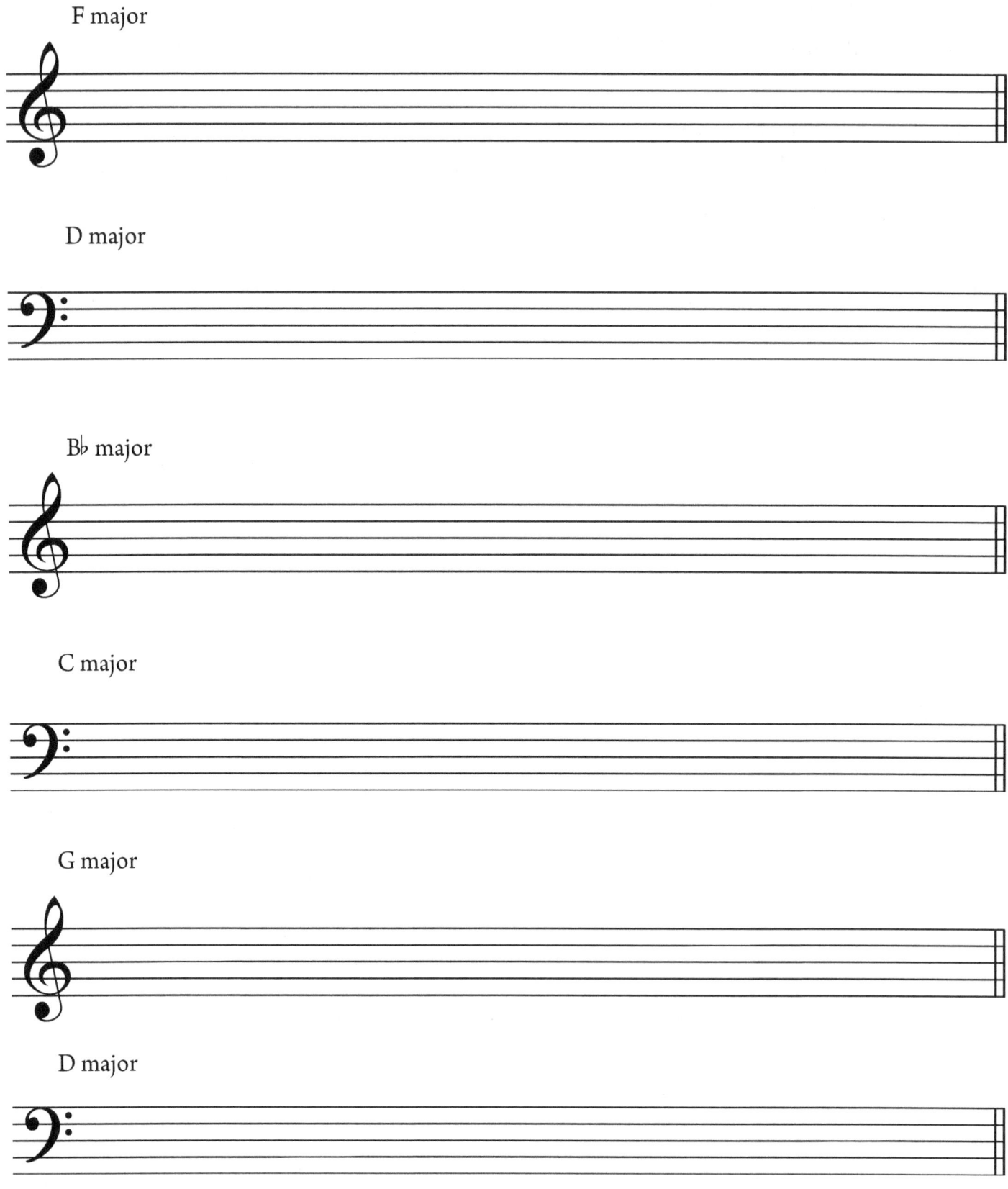

Scales Degrees

Each note of a scale can be given a number. This number is written with a small tent on top. This tent is called a caret ($\hat{1}$).

When a number has a caret on top, it refers to scale degree, which is just the number of the note as it occurs in the order of the scale. The first note is scale degree $\hat{1}$, the second is scale degree $\hat{2}$, etc.

The G major scale is shown below with scale degree numbers.

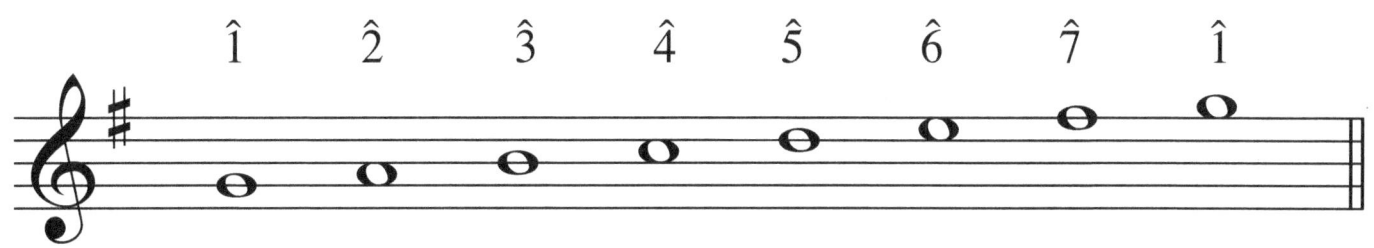

1. The notes below are all from the C major scale. Write the scale degree numbers above each note.

2. The notes below are all from the D major scale. Write the scale degree numbers above each note.

Minor Scales

A major scale evokes a particular color or character in sound. A minor scale has a different color or character. Some might say it has a sadder or darker sound, but that is a matter of opinion. The minor scale is another important scale in music, and it occurs frequently.

Every major key has a relative minor. They are related because they share the same key signature. C major's relative minor is A minor. Both keys have no sharps and flats in their key signatures.

The relative minor can be found three half steps below the major key. On the keyboard below you can see the first half step from C to B, the second half step from B to B♭, and the third half step from B♭ to A.

Keys of C major and A minor

3 half steps lower

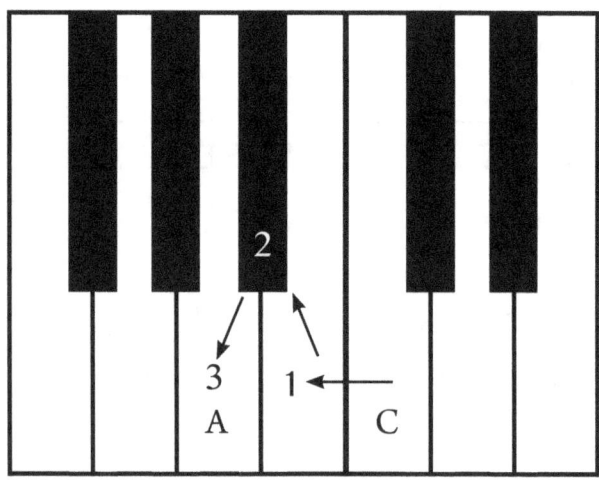

G major's relative minor is E minor. E is three half steps below G. They both share the same key signature of one sharp (F#).

Keys of G major and E minor

3 half steps lower

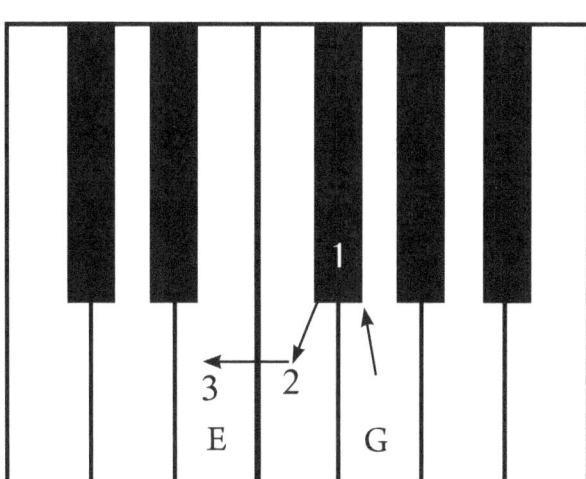

Here are the relative major and minor keys up to two sharps and two flats.

Major Key	Key Signature	Minor Key
C major	(no # or ♭)	A minor
G major	(F#)	E minor
D major	(F#, C#)	B minor
F major	(B♭)	D minor
B♭ major	(B♭, E♭)	G minor

Count down three half steps from the tonic of a major scale to find the relative minor key.

The Natural Minor Scale

The natural minor scale is a minor scale that uses the same key signature as its relative major.

The C major scale and the A natural minor scale have no sharps or flats.

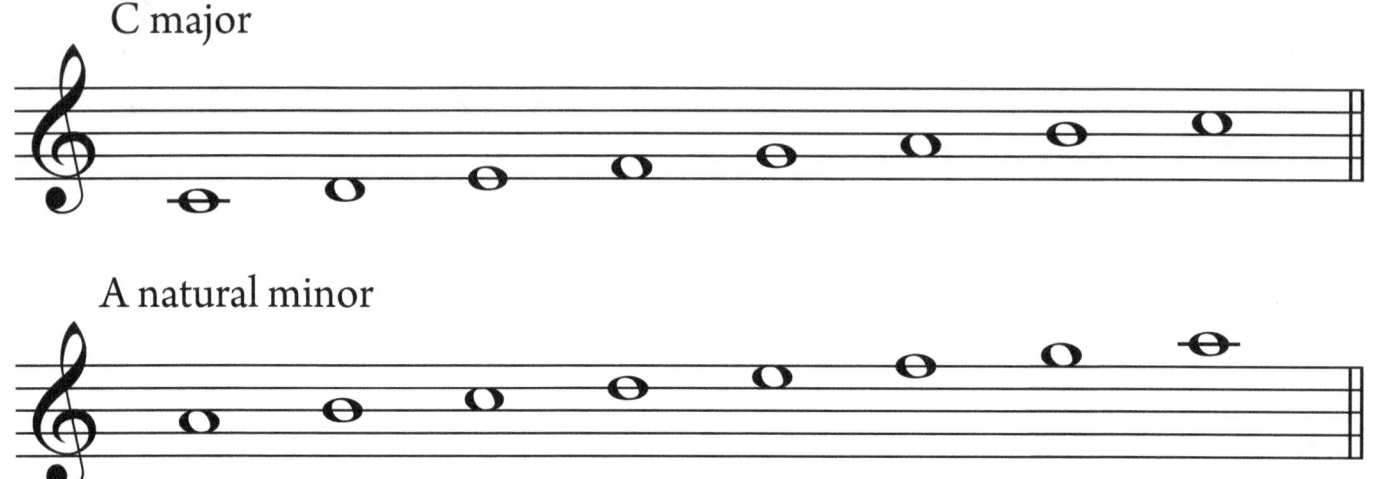

Since the G major scale and the E natural minor scale are relatives they each use the same key signature of one sharp (F♯).
To write the E natural minor scale just write a scale from E to E using the same key signature as G major (F♯).

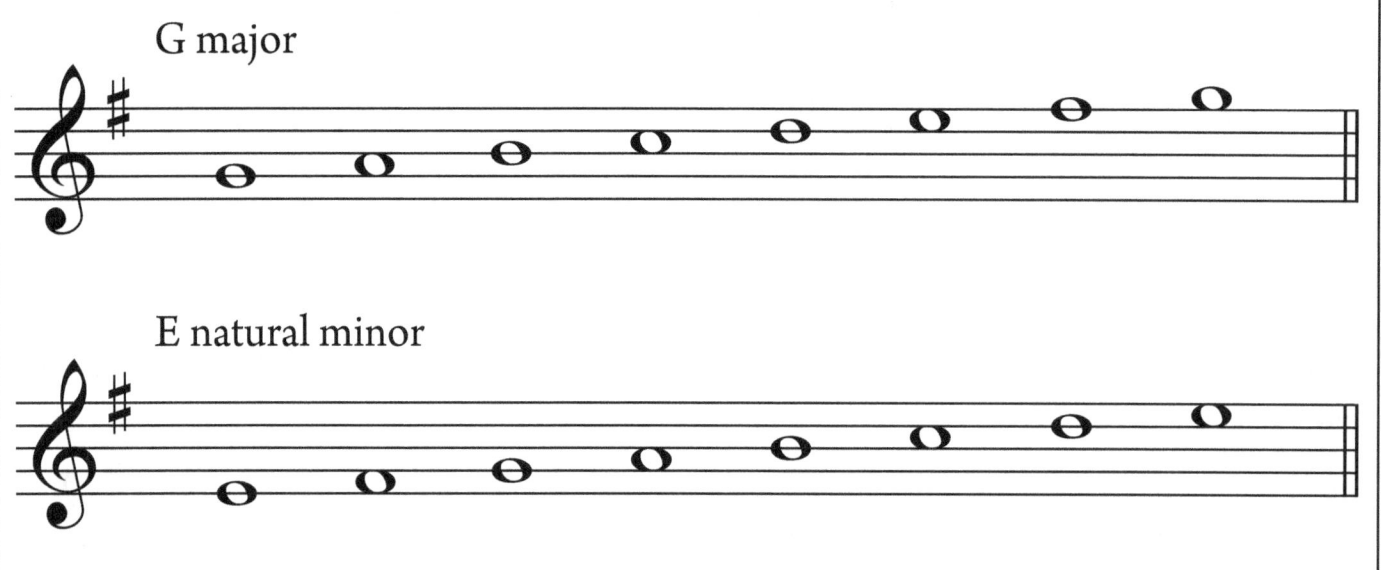

1. Name the relative minor keys for the following major keys.

        C major   _____

        D major   _____

        F major   _____

        G major   _____

        B♭ major   _____

2. Write the following key signatures on the grand staves.

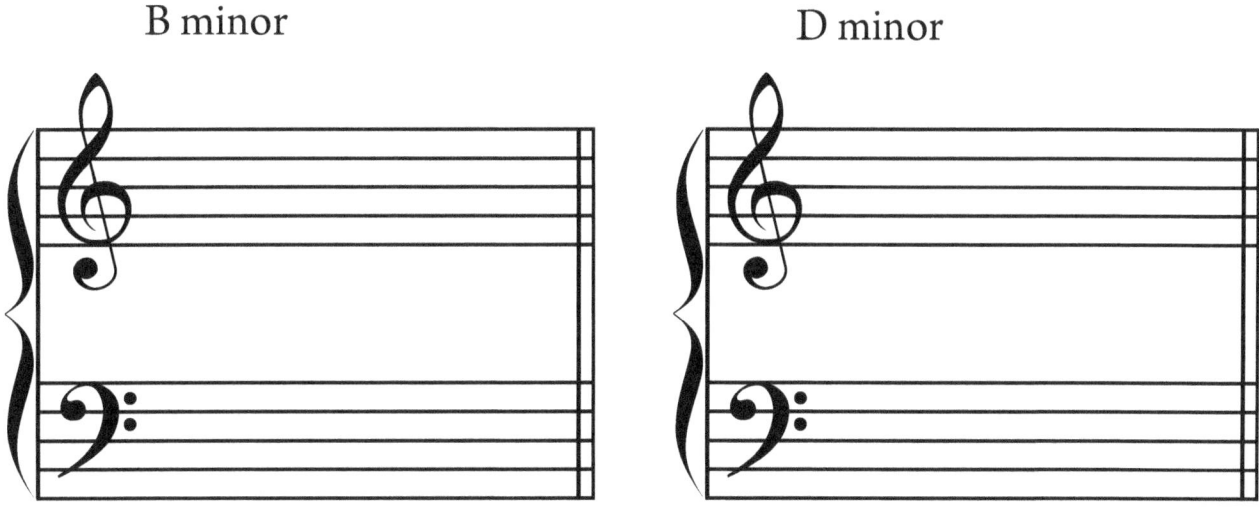

3. Write the following scales ascending and descending using key signatures and whole notes.

E natural minor

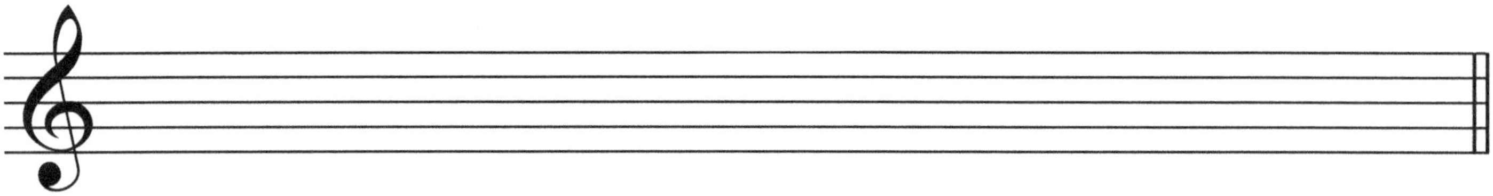

G natural minor

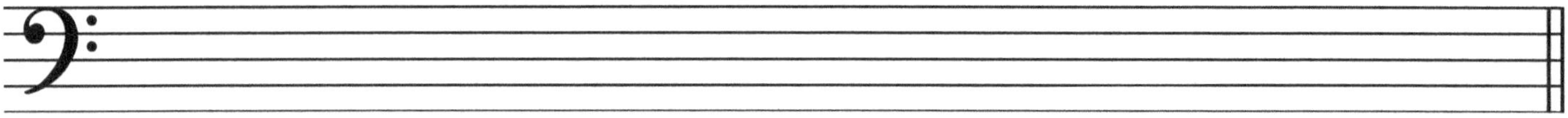

D natural minor

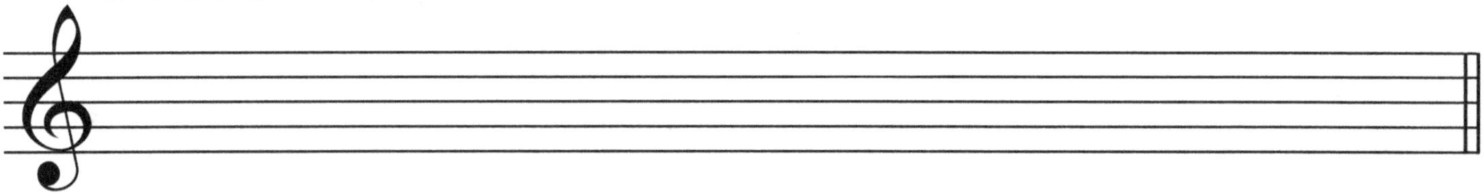

B natural minor

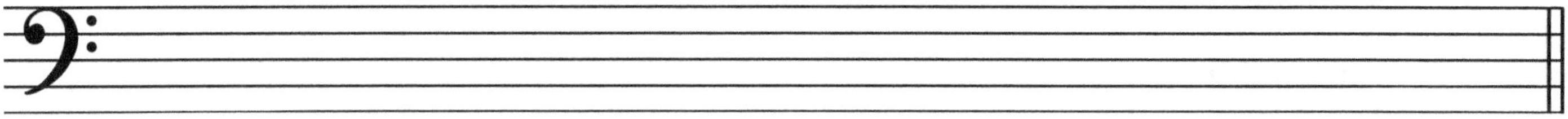

A natural minor

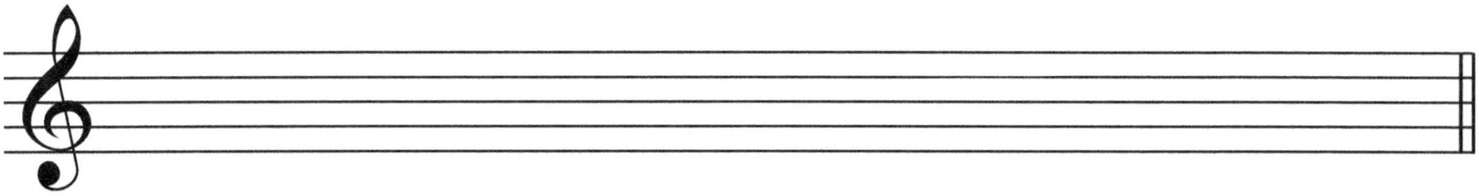

The Harmonic Minor Scale

The harmonic minor scale is the natural minor scale with scale degree $\hat{7}$ raised one half step.

The example below shows the A harmonic minor scale. It is the natural minor scale with scale degree $\hat{7}$ raised one half step from G to G♯.

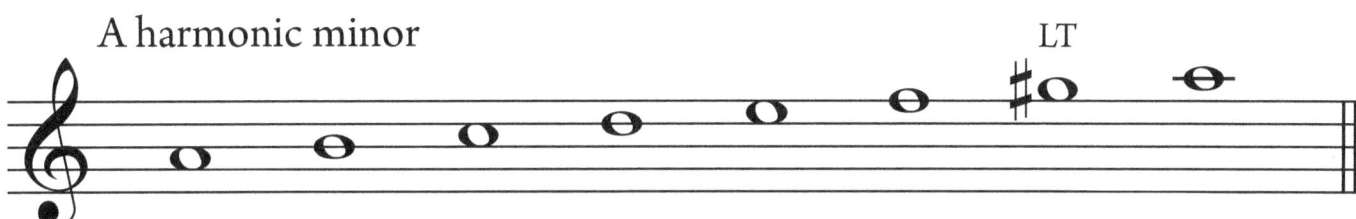

The example below shows the E harmonic minor scale ascending and descending. Since its relative major is G major it has a key signature with one sharp (F♯) and it also has raised $\hat{7}$ (D♯).
Since the scale is written in one measure, the D stays sharp in the descending part of the scale.

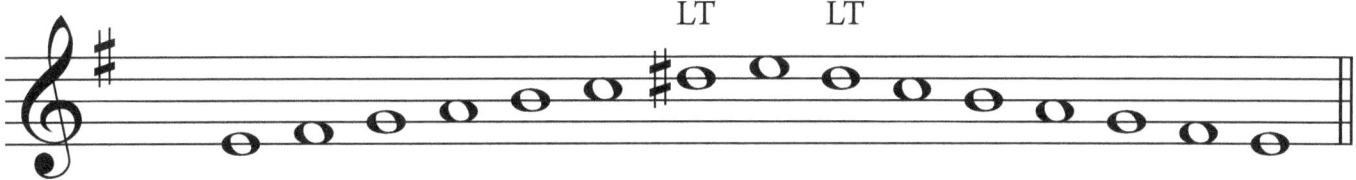

The Leading Tone

Scale degree one ($\hat{1}$) is called the tonic and scale degree five ($\hat{5}$) is called the dominant. Scale degree $\hat{7}$ is called the leading tone (LT). The leading tone is a half step away from the tonic and because of this it pulls or "leads" to the tonic. The leading tone occurs in major and harmonic minor scales. Play a scale and stop on scale degree $\hat{7}$. Hear how it wants to "lead" to the tonic.

1. Write the following scales ascending and descending using key signatures and whole notes. Label the leading tones (LT).

E harmonic minor

G harmonic minor

D harmonic minor

B harmonic minor

A harmonic minor

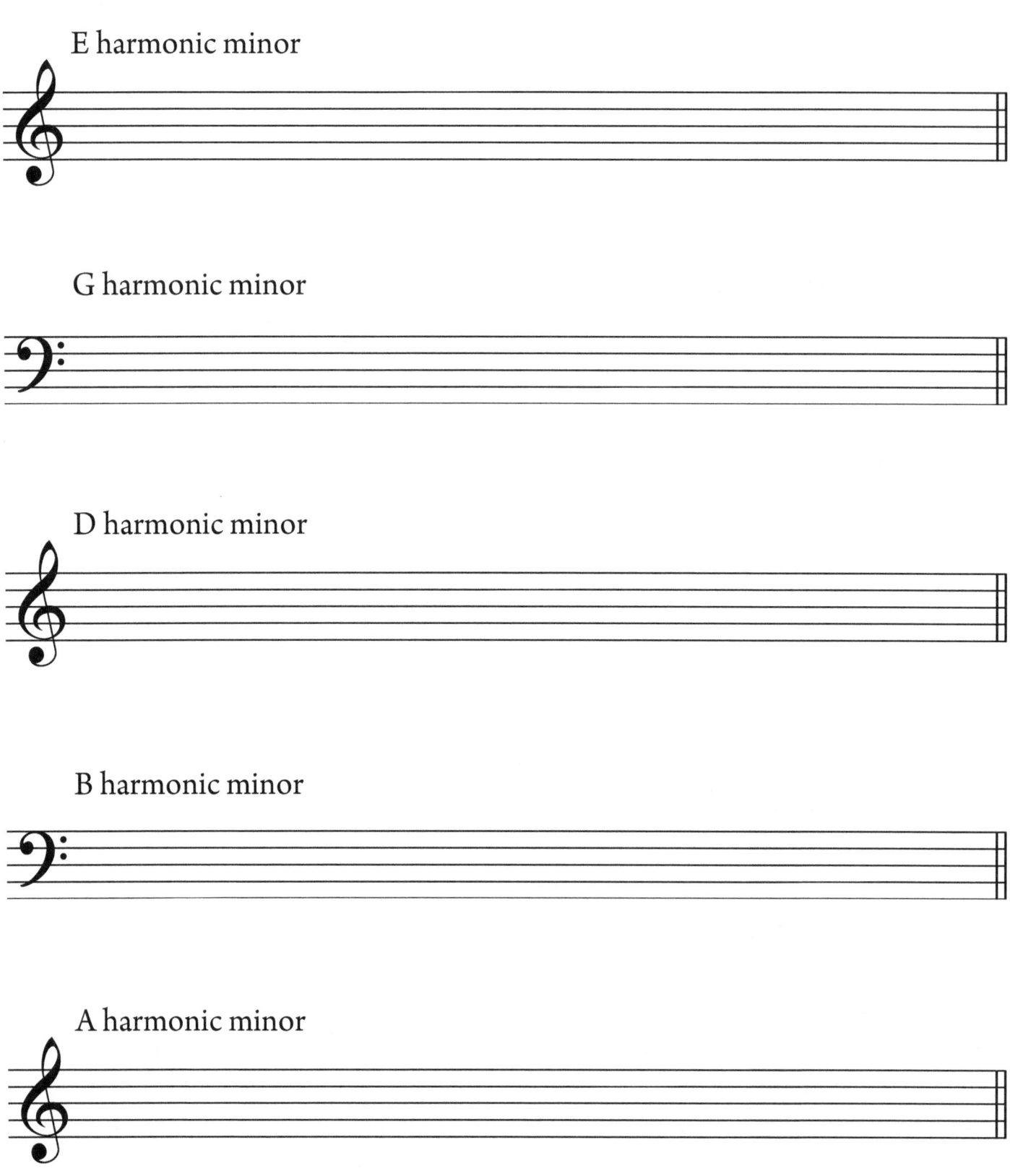

The Melodic Minor Scale

The melodic minor scale is the natural minor scale with scale degree $\hat{6}$ and $\hat{7}$ raised one half step ascending and $\hat{6}$ and $\hat{7}$ lowered one half step when it descends. It is different going up than it is going down.

The example below shows the D melodic minor scale. D minor has the same key signature as it's relative major, F major. When the scale goes up, B♭ is raised to B♮ and C is raised to C♯. When the scale goes down, C♯ is lowered to C♮ and B♮ is lowered to B♭.

The Leading Tone and the Subtonic

When scale degree $\hat{7}$ is one half step from the tonic it is called the leading tone. In two scales, the natural minor, and the descending melodic minor, $\hat{7}$ is a whole step away from the tonic.

In this case, being a whole step away, it does not "lead" to the tonic and is called the subtonic.

The example below show the G minor melodic scale. The ascending form of the scale contains the leading tone (LT), and the descending form of the scale contains the subtonic (ST).

1. Write the following scales ascending and descending using key signatures and whole notes. Label the leading tones (LT) and the subtonic notes (ST).

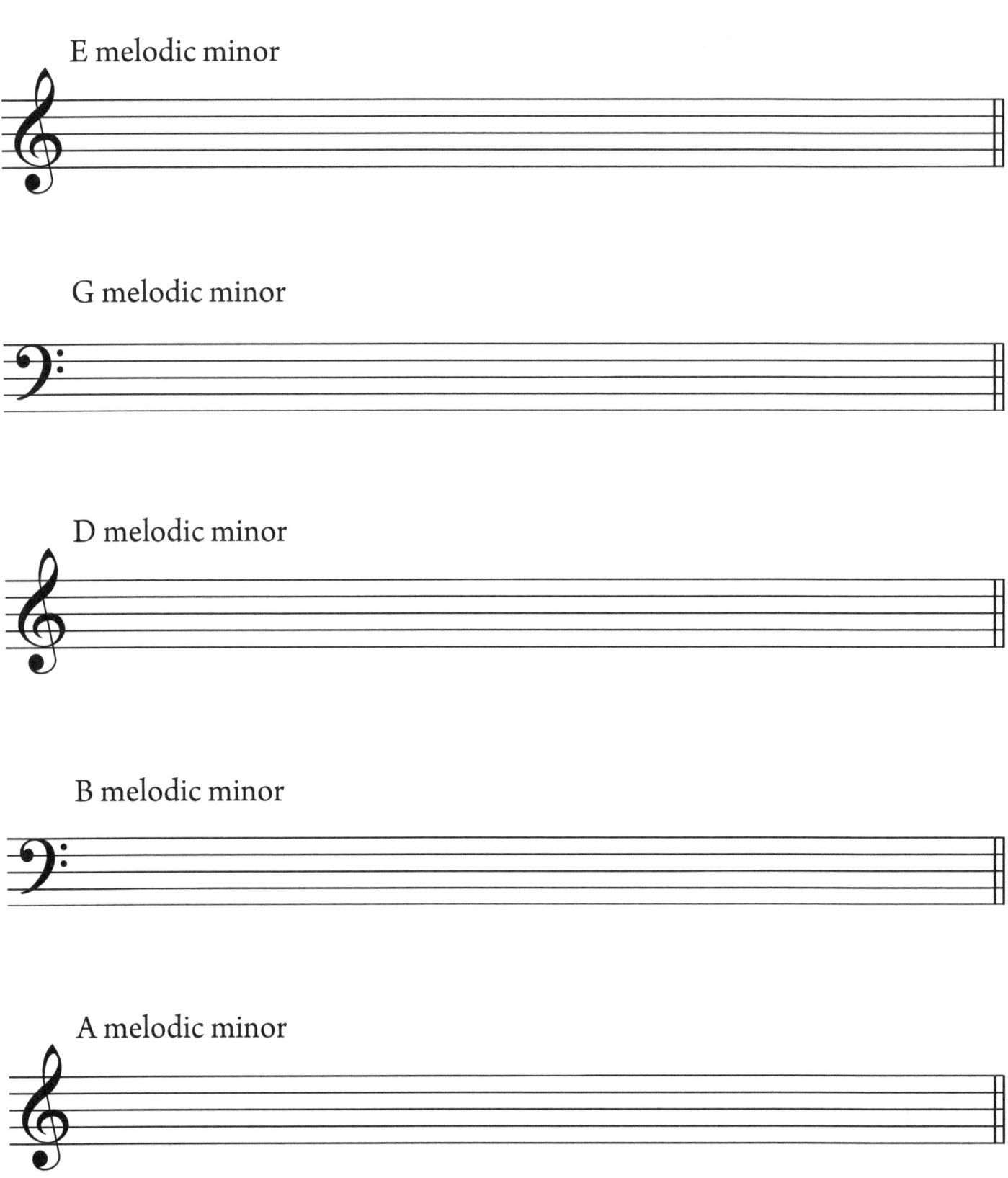

The String Section

The sound of the string instrument is created by vibrating strings. These strings are stretched across the hollow body of an instrument and most are played by plucking or drawing a bow across them. String instruments include the:

violin
viola
cello
double bass
harp
guitar

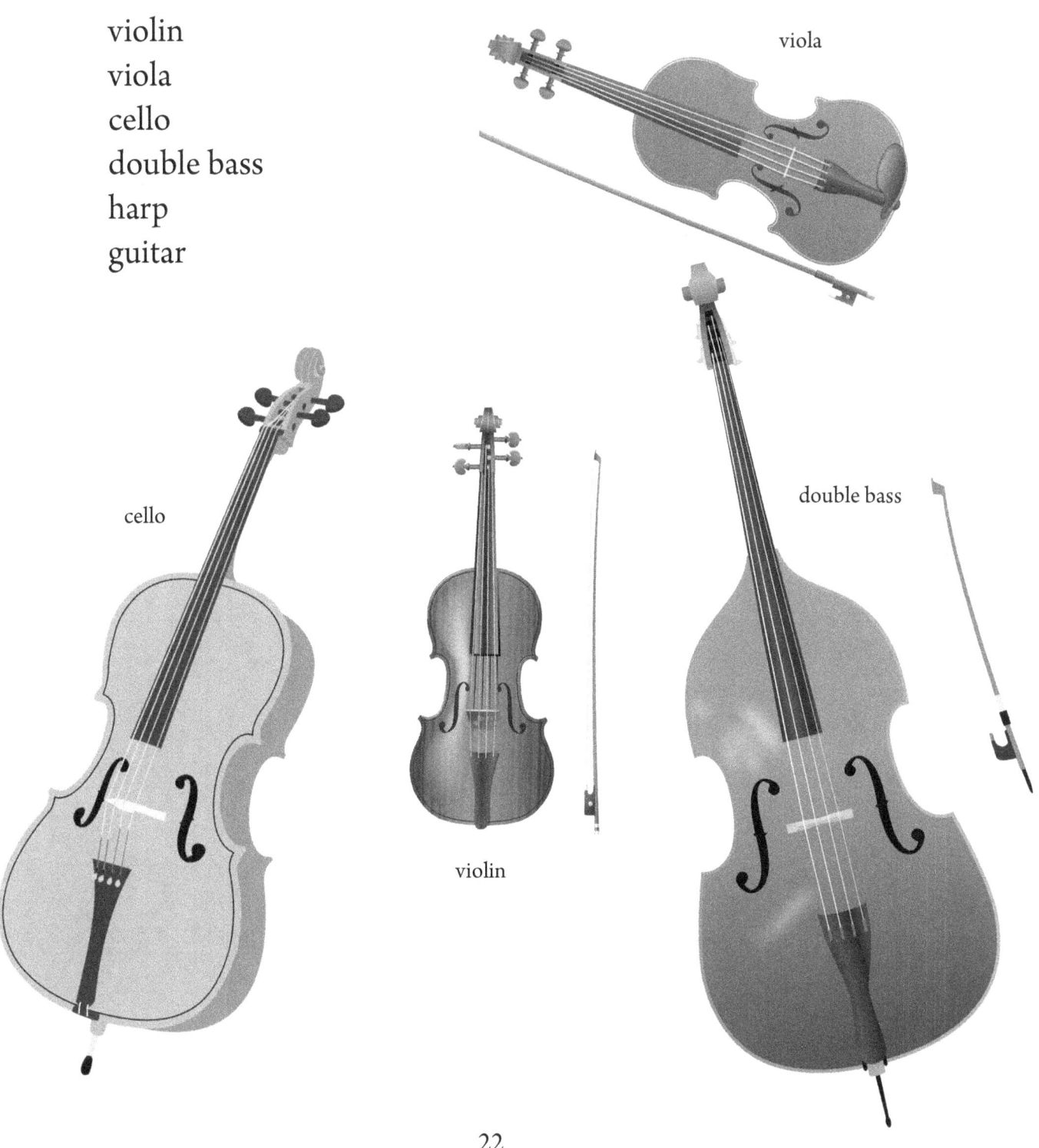

Half Steps and Accidentals

A half step is the shortest distance between two notes.
An accidental is a sign placed in front of a note that changes the pitch of the note by raising or lowering it.

A sharp (♯) raises a note by one half step.
A flat (♭) lowers a note by one half step.
A natural (♮) cancels a sharp or a flat.

With the use of accidentals, it is possible for a single pitch to have two different names. For example, F sharp and G flat are two different names for the same pitch, or the same key on the keyboard.
The same is true for A sharp and B flat. Play an A sharp and a B flat on your instrument. Do they sound the same?

When we change the name of a note without changing its pitch,
this change is called an enharmonic change.

1. Give another name for the following notes.

G♯ _____   E♭ _____

B♭ _____   F♭ _____

D♯ _____   B♯ _____

A♭ _____   F♯ _____

C♯ _____   D♭ _____

Chromatic Half Steps

A half step that consists of two notes with the same letter name is called a chromatic half step.

Here are four examples of chromatic half steps.

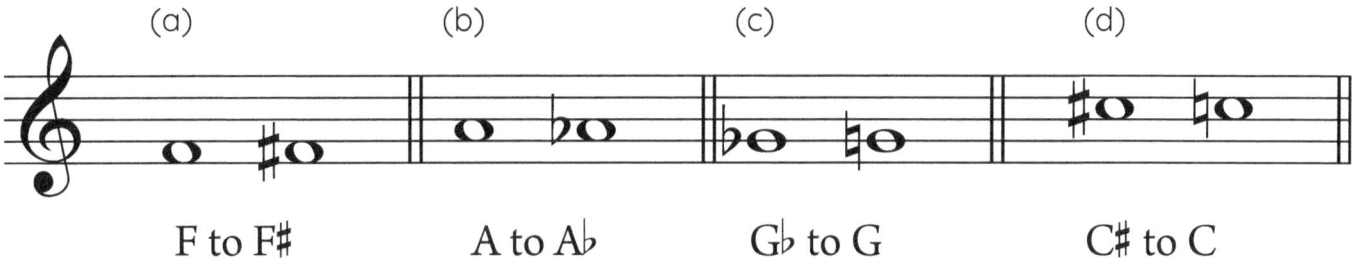

(a) F to F#   (b) A to A♭   (c) G♭ to G   (d) C# to C

(a) A sharp raises a natural one half step.
(b) A flat lowers a natural one half step.
(c) A natural raises a flat one half step.
(d) A natural lowers a sharp one half step.

1. Write chromatic half steps above the following notes.

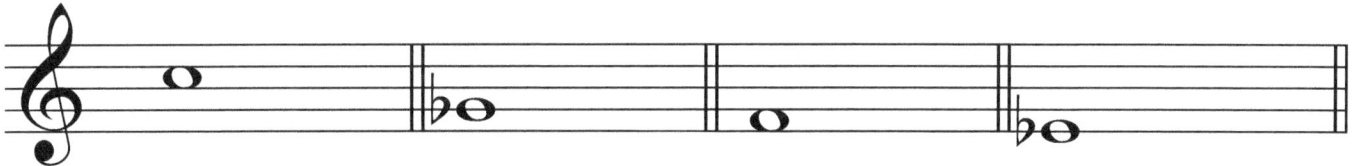

2. Write chromatic half steps below the following notes.

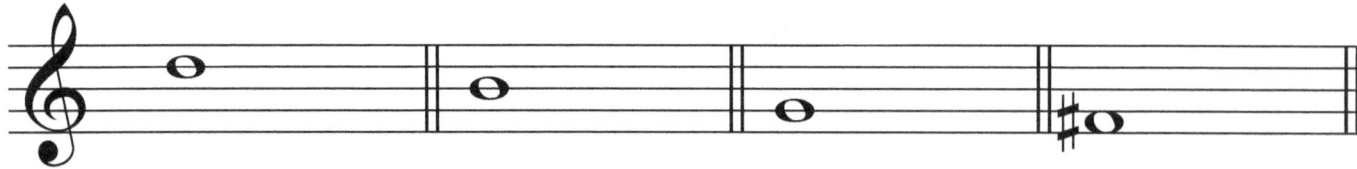

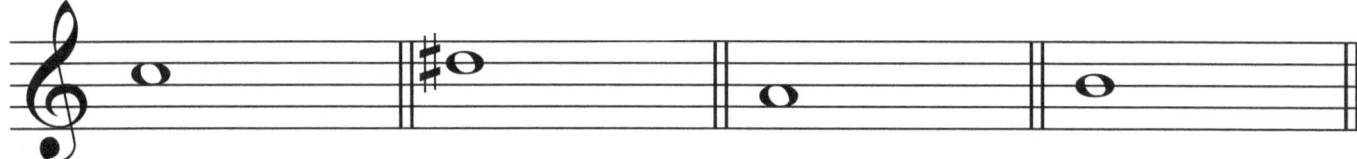

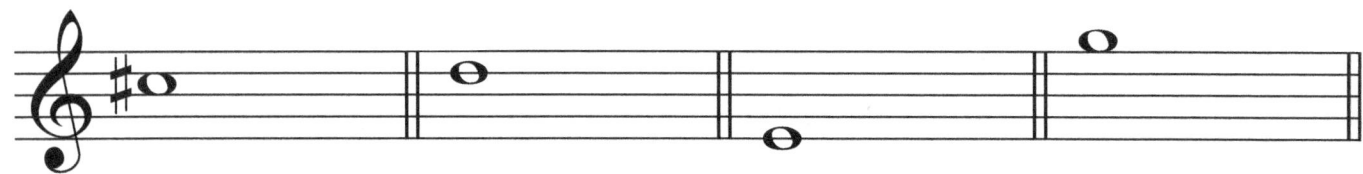

Diatonic Half Steps

A half step that consists of two notes with different letter names is called a diatonic half step.

Here are four examples of diatonic half steps.

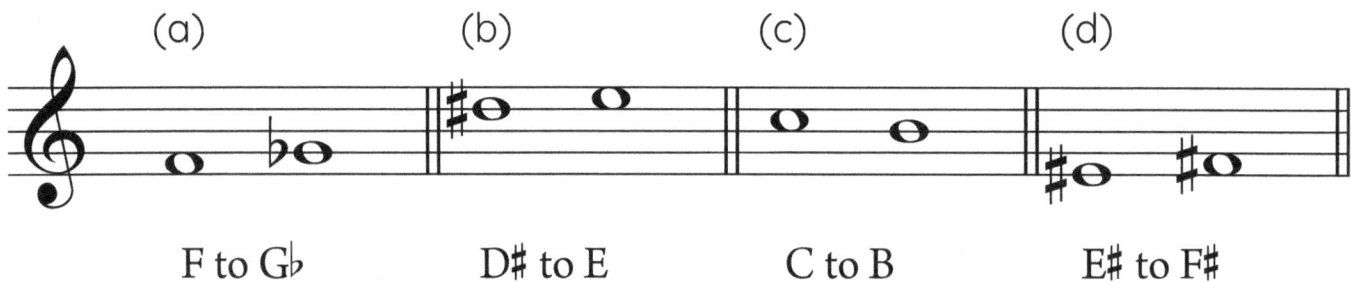

(a) F to G♭ (b) D♯ to E (c) C to B (d) E♯ to F♯

Remember that a whole step is made up of two half steps.

On the keyboard, a whole step is the distance between two keys with one key between them. Whole steps usually have two different letter names. For example, C to D, F sharp to G sharp, and A flat to B flat are all whole steps.

1. Write diatonic half steps above the following notes.

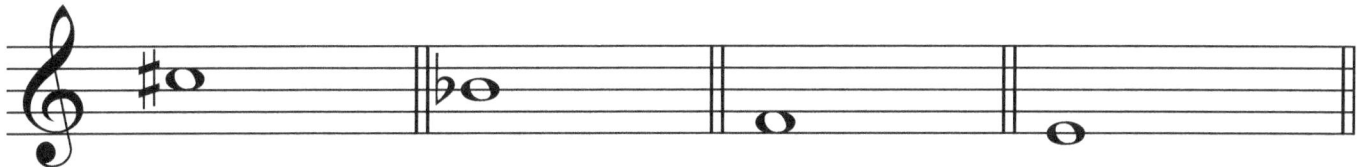

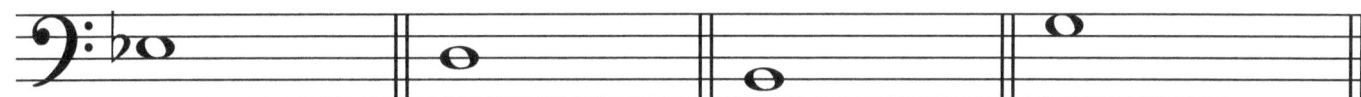

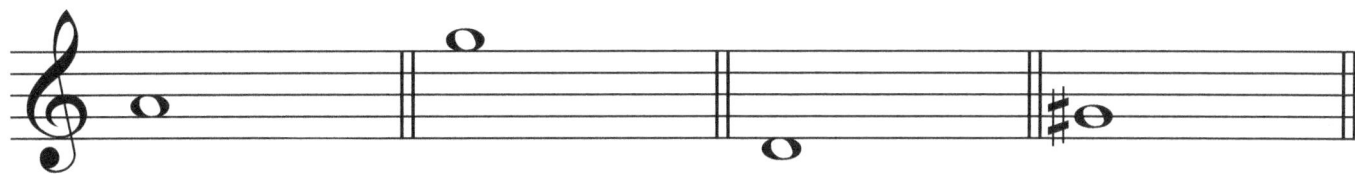

2. Write diatonic half steps below the following notes.

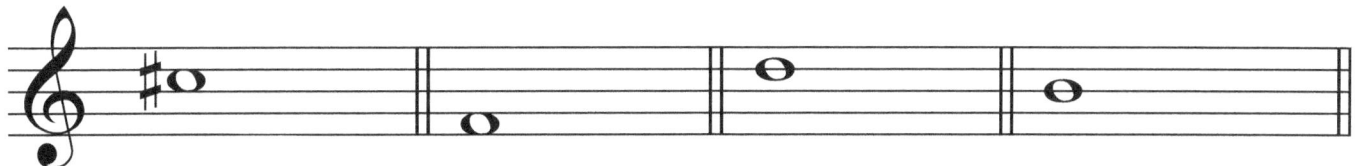

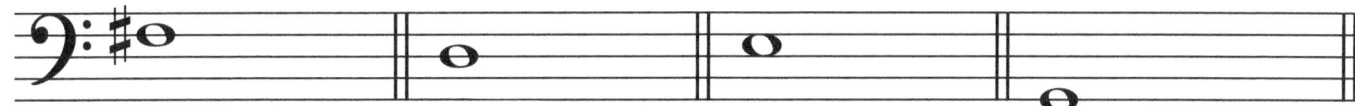

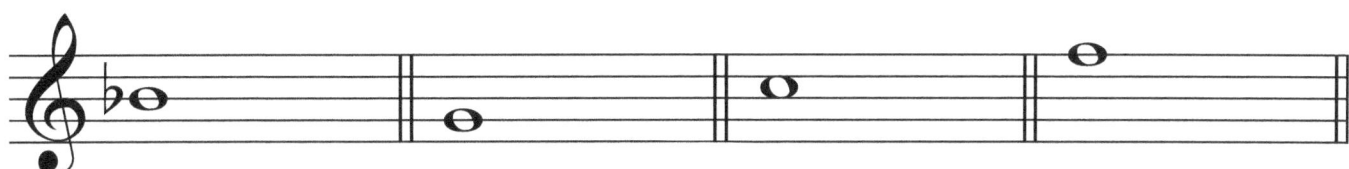

3. Mark the following intervals as chromatic half steps (C), diatonic half steps (D), or whole steps (W).

Italian Terms

a tempo — return to the original tempo
cantabile — in a singing style
dolce — sweetly
legato — smooth
M.D. mano destra — right hand
M.S. mano sinistra — left hand

Review Quiz 1

100

1. Name these notes.

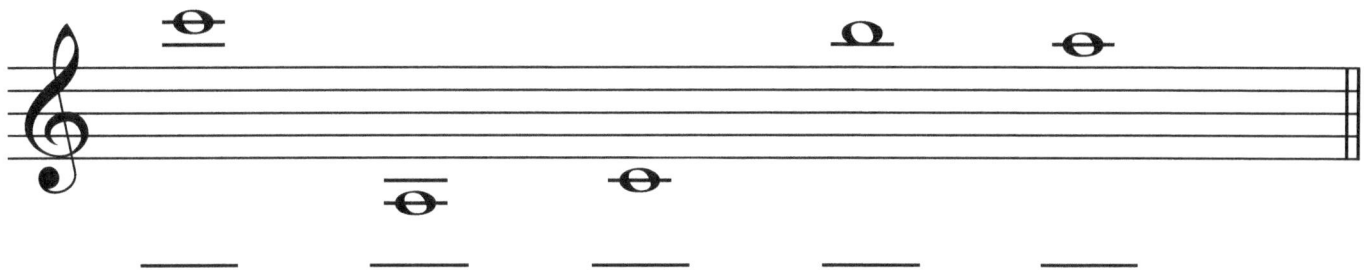

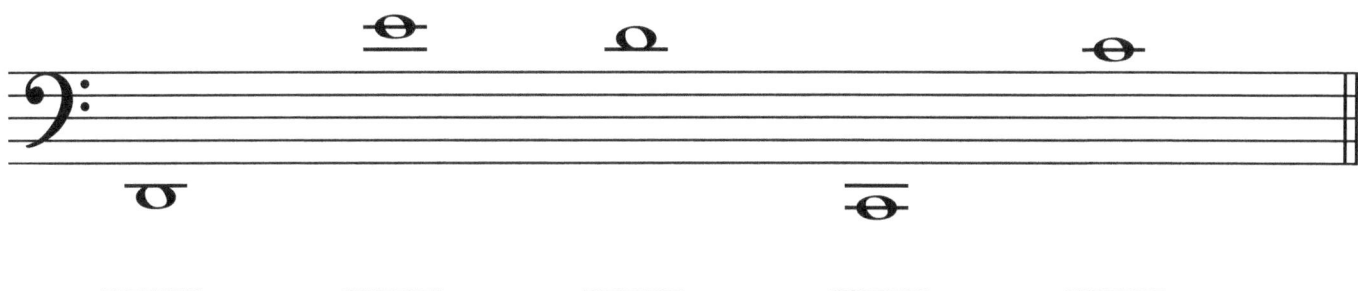

10

2. Name the relative minors of the following major keys.

        C major   ___ minor

        G major   ___ minor

        D major   ___ minor

        F major   ___ minor

        B♭ major   ___ minor

15

3. Write the follow scales ascending and descending using key signatures for each. Mark the leading tones with LT.

D major

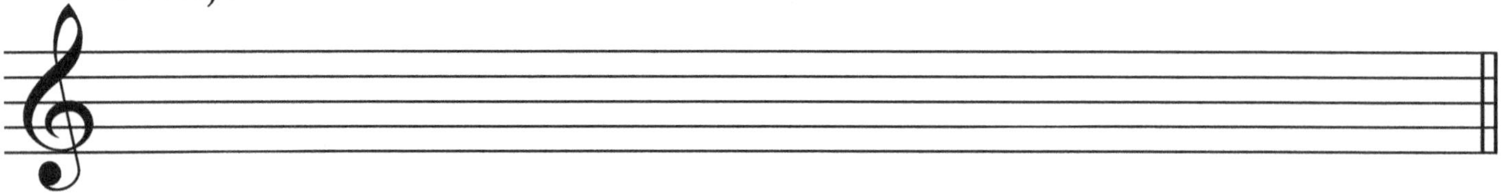

G natural minor

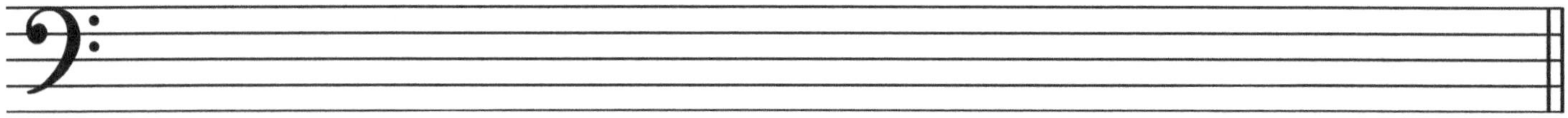

D harmonic minor

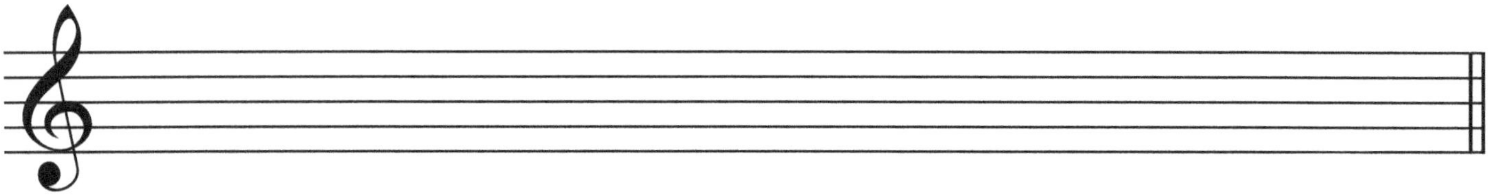

B melodic minor

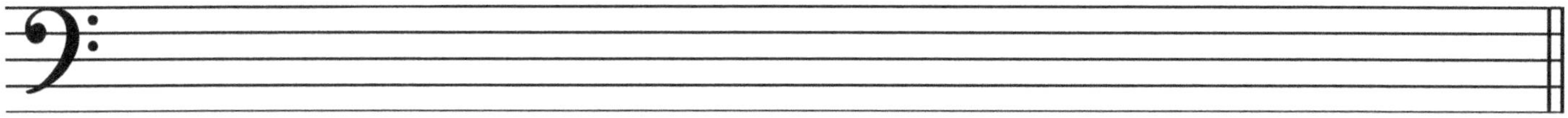

B flat major

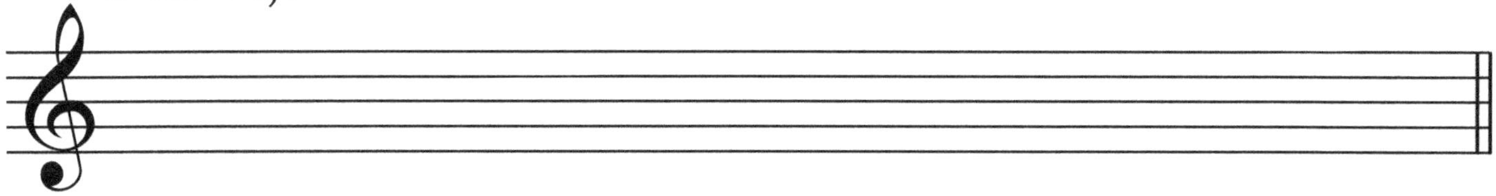

A harmonic minor

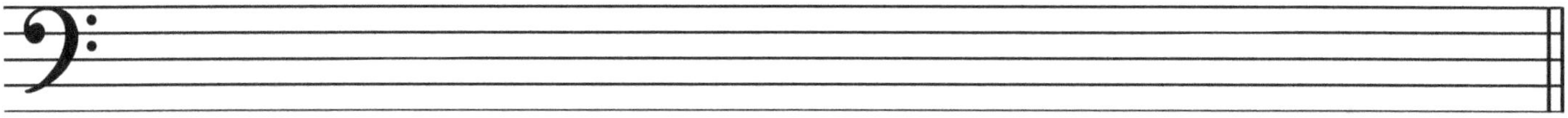

E melodic minor

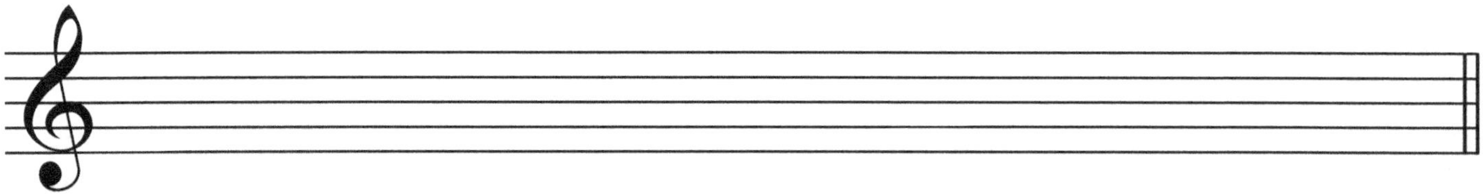

4. Write chromatic half steps above the following notes.

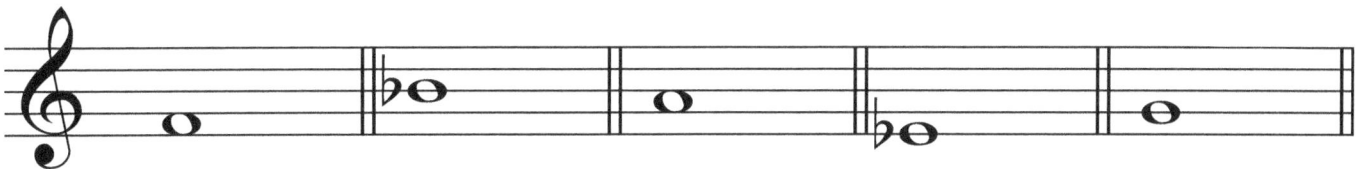

10

5. Write diatonic half steps below the following notes.

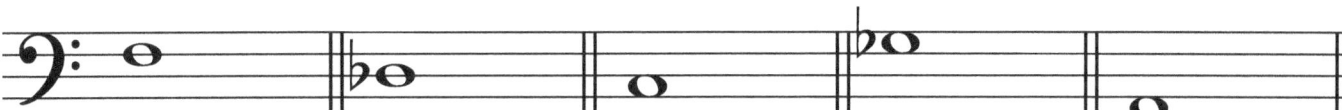

10

6. Write whole steps above the following notes.

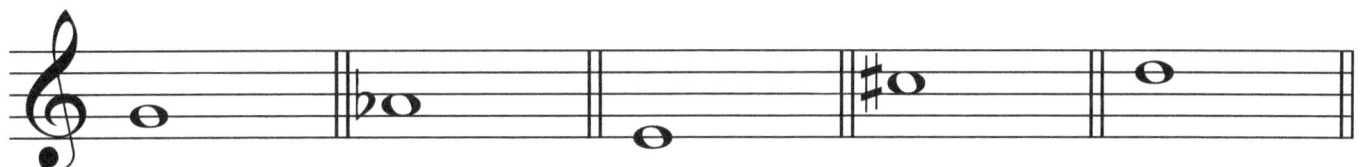

10

7. Write the Italian terms for the following definitions.

in a singing style   _____

sweetly   _____

left hand   _____

smooth   _____

return to the original tempo _____

10

Major and Perfect Intervals

An interval is the distance between two notes. There are several different types of intervals.

Here are the intervals that are formed between the bottom note and all the other notes of major scale.

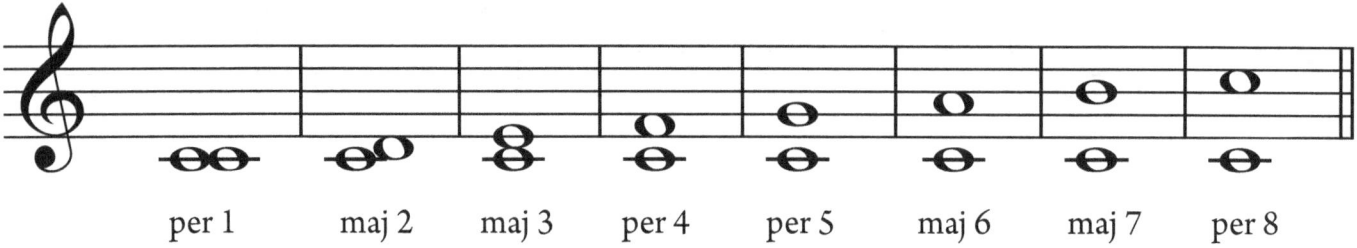

per 1   maj 2   maj 3   per 4   per 5   maj 6   maj 7   per 8

The intervals of a unison (1), 4th, 5th, and octave (8) are classified as perfect intervals.

The intervals of a 2nd, 3rd, 6th, and 7th are classified as major intervals.

Think of the bottom note of an interval as the tonic of a major scale.

If the upper note of the interval is a member of the scale of the lower note, the interval will be either perfect or major.

G to C is a perfect 4th because C is the fourth note of the G major scale.

G to F sharp is a major 7th because F sharp is the seventh note of the G major scale.

1. Write the scale of D major using accidentals.

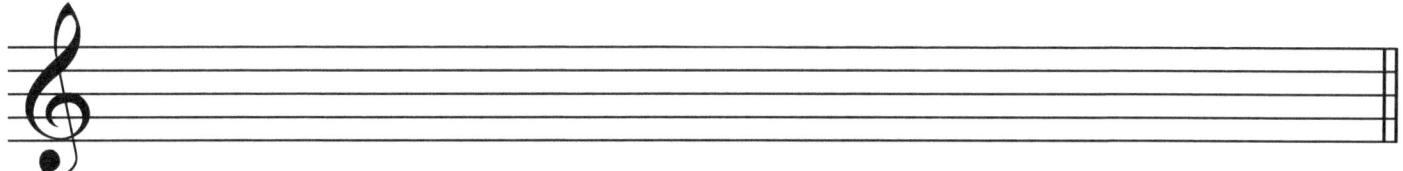

2. Write the following intervals above the note D.

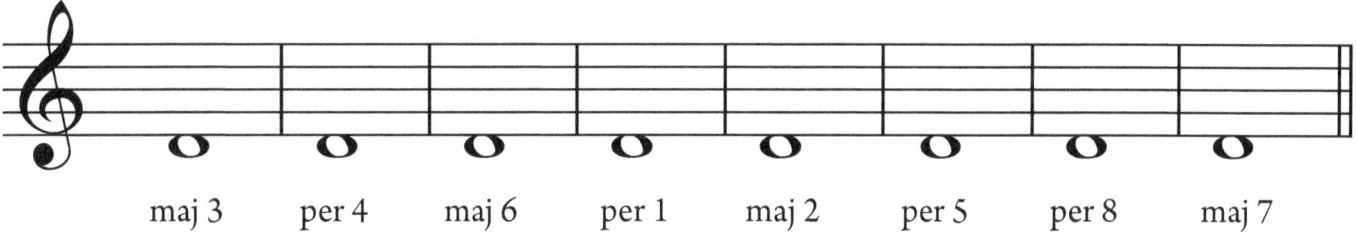

3. Write the scale of F major using accidentals.

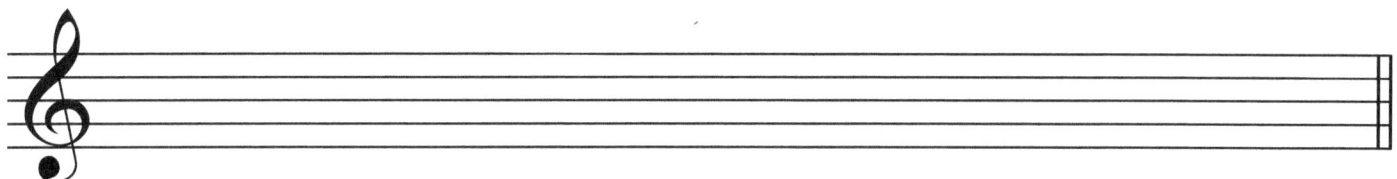

4. Write the following intervals above the note F.

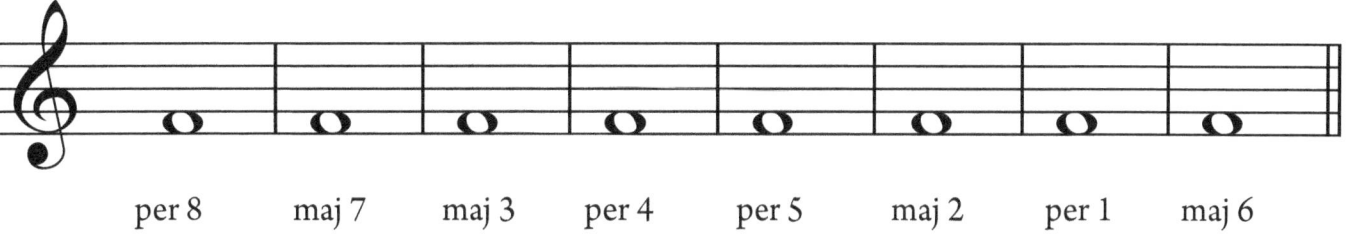

5. Write the scale of B flat major using accidentals.

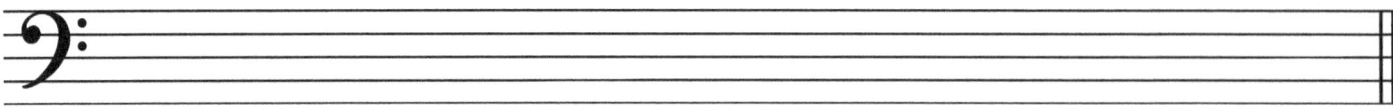

6. Write the following intervals above the note B flat.

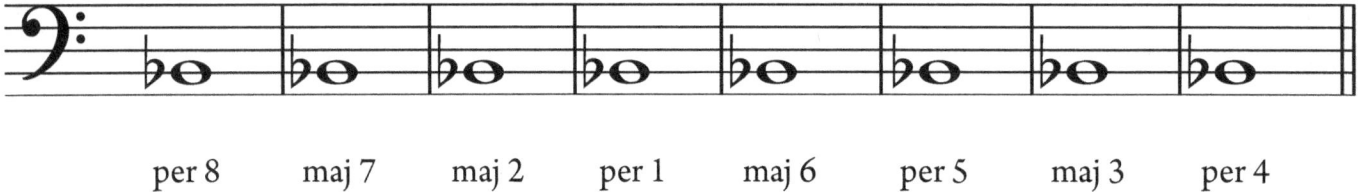

per 8   maj 7   maj 2   per 1   maj 6   per 5   maj 3   per 4

7. Write the scale of G major using accidentals.

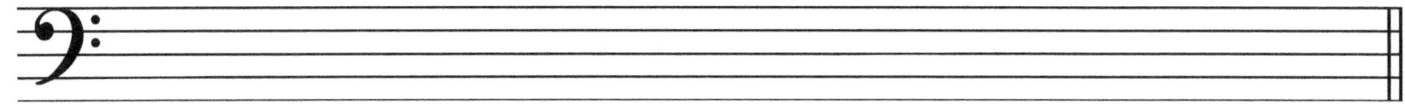

8. Write the following intervals above the note G.

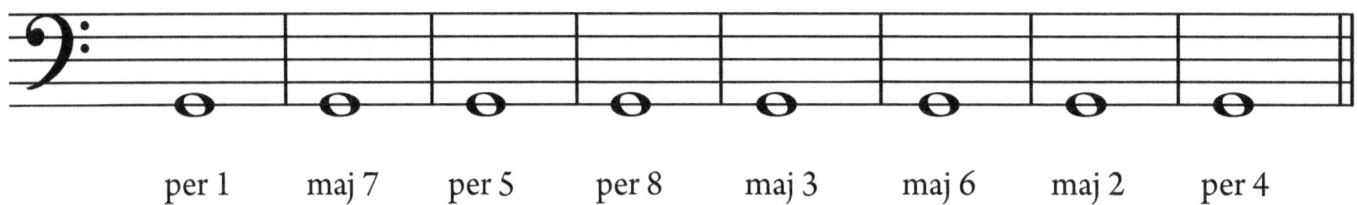

per 1   maj 7   per 5   per 8   maj 3   maj 6   maj 2   per 4

9. Name the following intervals.

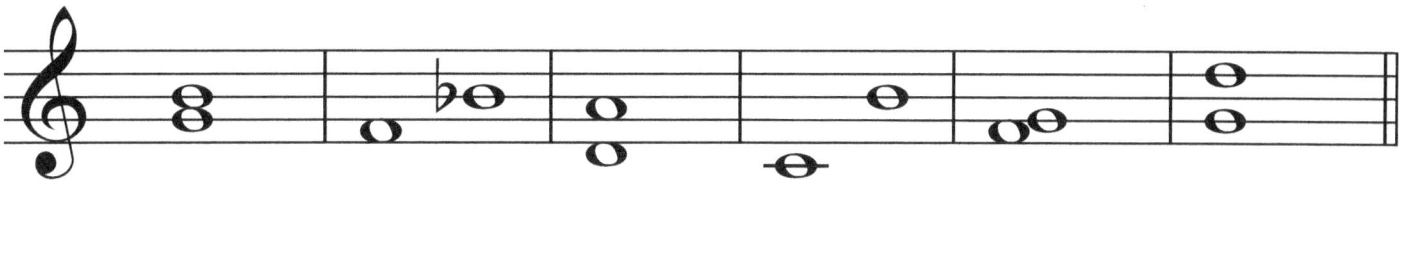

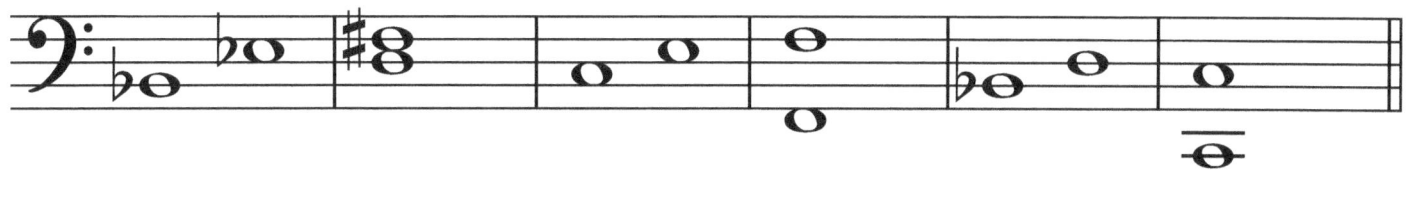

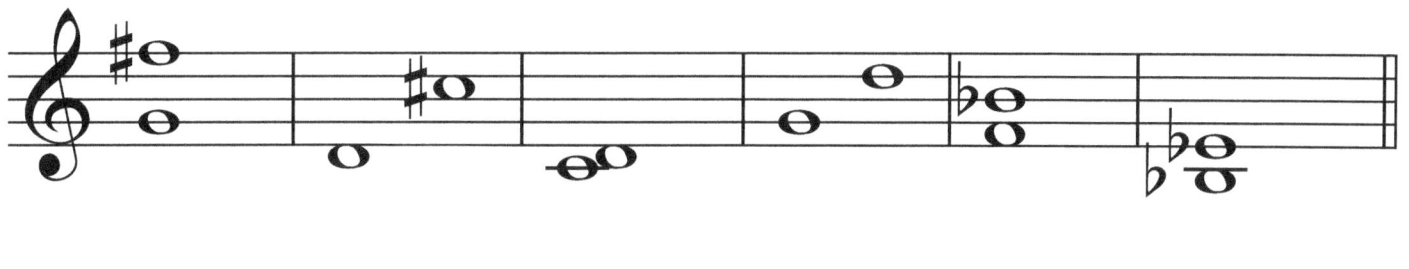

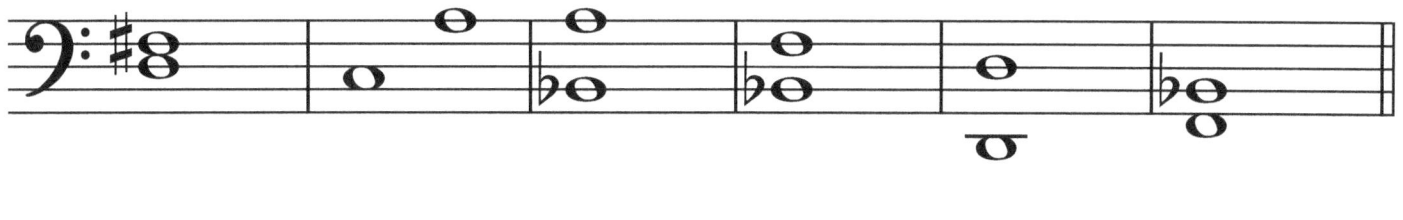

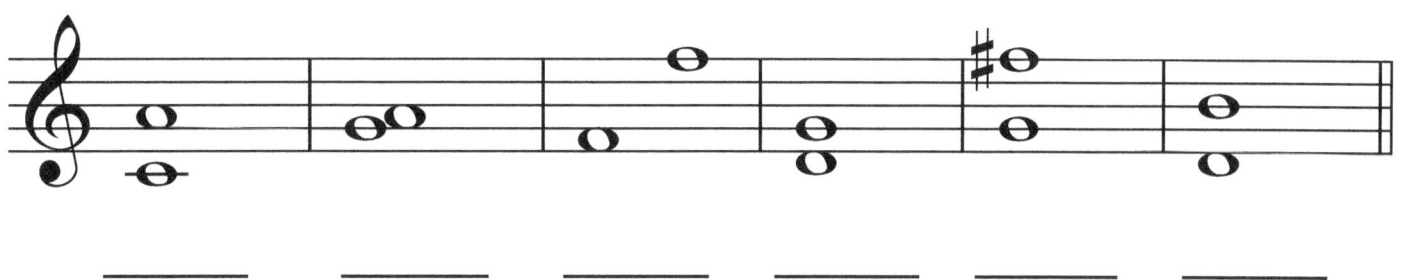

Review

Fill in the blanks using words from the list below.

(a) Small lines called _____ are used to extend the range of the staff.

(b) A _____ is the shortest distance between two notes.

(c) An _____ is a sign placed in front of a note that changes its pitch by raising or lowering it.

(d) A _____ raises a note by one half step.

(e) A _____ lowers a note by one half step.

(f) A _____ cancels a sharp or flat.

(g) A half step that consists of two notes with the same letter name is called a _____.

(h) A half step that consists of two notes with different letter names is called a _____.

(i) A _____ is made up of two half steps.

(j) An _____ is the distance between two notes.

    interval   half step
    whole step   sharp
    flat   natural
    accidental   chromatic half step
    ledger lines   diatonic half step

```
S H S P J J S T H F R A C S M K V A V S
L M Z H I D V X P V S V D P V K M E I V
L A H C E L L O J E H C T I L D H C O Z
C N A B B S C A L E X N G D J X Z Q L V
L O R H G P H C K V P G Z O X N D N I V
A D M H A L F S T E P L H J E K X A N E
R E O E U J D H J X D Q Z M L B H T V N
I S N R E L A T I V E M A J O R A U Q M
N T I X O B O E T E Z X L U X Z C R L E
E R C O Q O V I O L A D U Y V V O A M L
T A P Y A K C D V L O O W B D G M L W O
U X D N S A R F Z H I U U U P C P C C D
S H I O L S H A R P Y B I Y X H O U L I
N V A F U L E D G E R L I N E R S K E C
O A T V R J E V I N A E A H T O E N F V
T L O P B R X M B H F B D M H M R L H D
E I N W O C T N C X L A O G L A S K L D
E S I D N G N I H L A S L S L T U X R M
L I C O G G F H L Y T S C E J I U Q G W
W E Y O C A N T A B I L E S L C J J V P
```

clef
chromatic
flat
dolce
note
scale
relative major
oboe

slur
diatonic
natural
mano destra
violin
cello
melodic
clarinet

half step
sharp
cantabile
composers
ledger line
double bass
harmonic
viola

The Brass Section

Brass instruments are really made of brass. They are long tubes of curled up metal with flared ends called bells. You play a brass instrument by buzzing your lips into a mouthpiece. This makes air vibrate through the tubes and creates sound.

The main instruments of the brass family are:

trumpet
horn
trombone
tuba

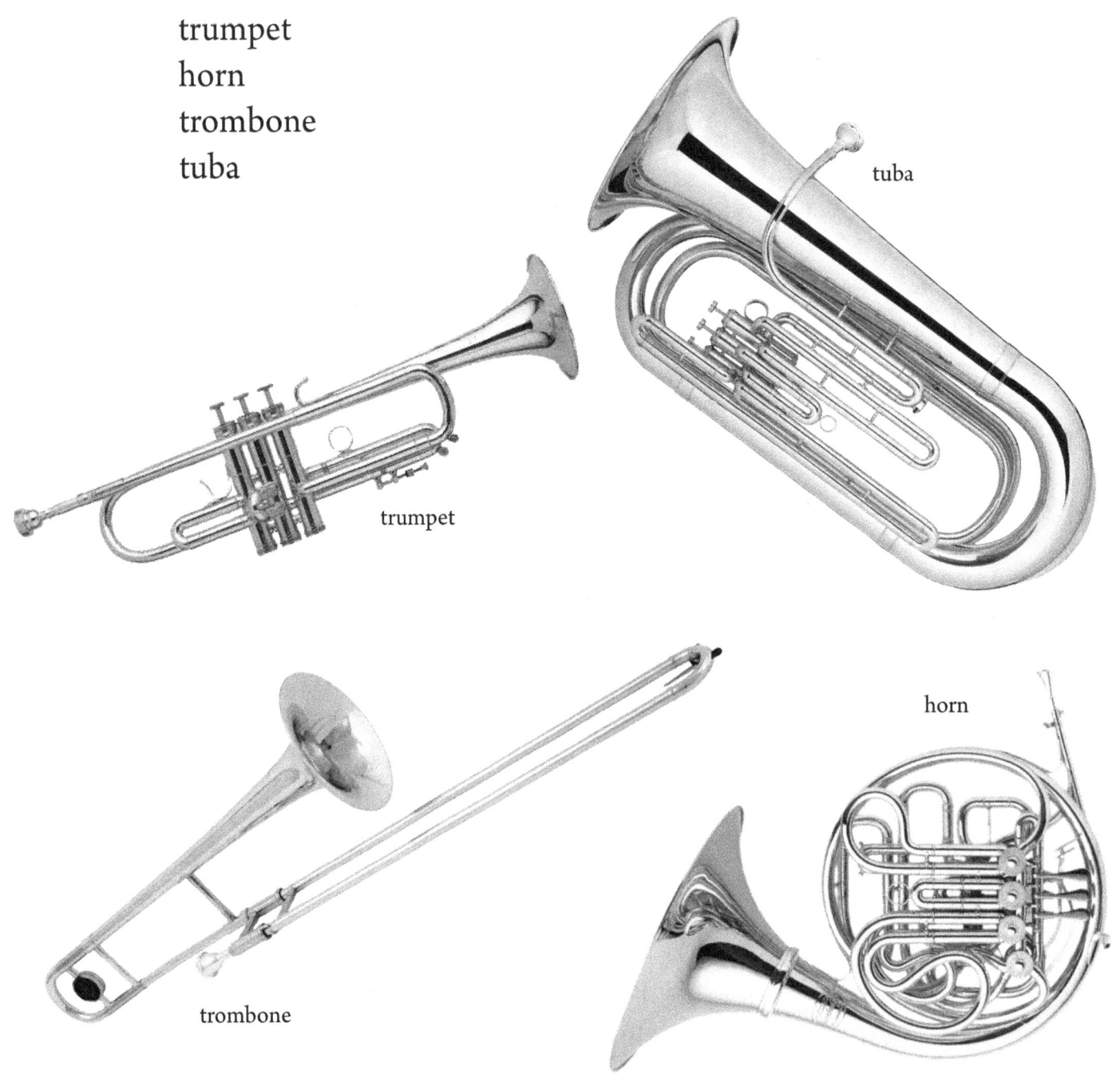

Time Signature Review

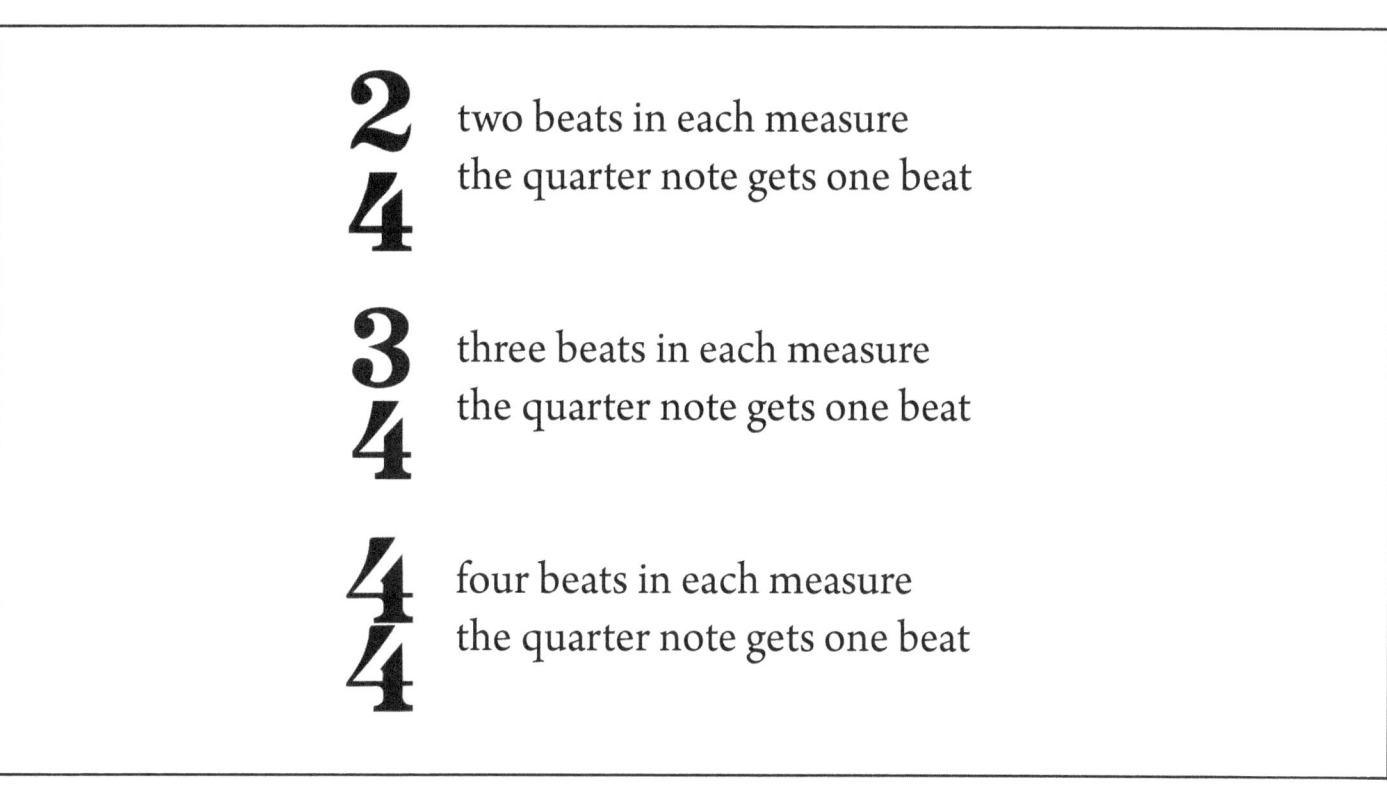

1. Add time signatures to the following rhythms.

Dotted Quarter Notes

A dot adds one half the value to the original note.

In 2/4, 3/4 and 4/4, the quarter note receives one beat.

This means that a dot after a quarter note will add half a beat to the quarter note.

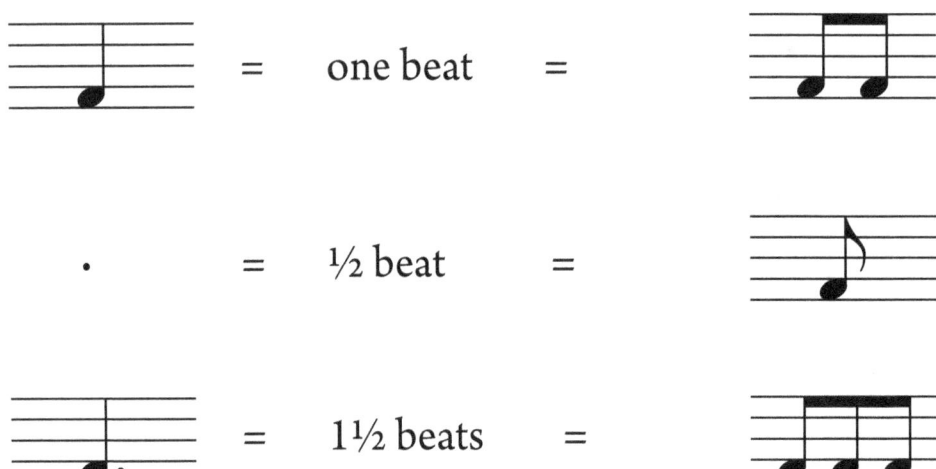

A dotted quarter is equal to a quarter note tied to an eighth note.

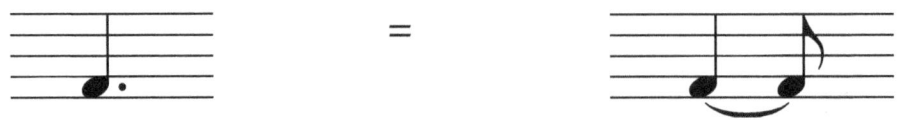

Here is one way to count a dotted quarter note.

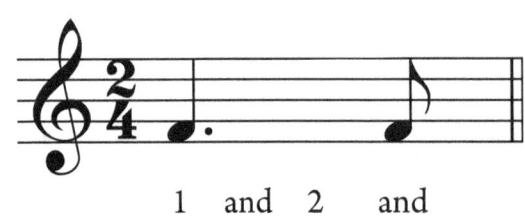

1. Add bar lines to these rhythms according to the time signatures.

Sixteenth Notes

A sixteenth note looks like an eighth note with an extra flag on its stem.

Two or more sixteenth notes are joined together by two beams.

Two sixteenth notes equal one eighth note.

Four sixteenth notes equal one quarter note.

Counting Sixteenth Notes

The beat can be divided into four when we play sixteenth notes. When counting, it helps to say 1 ee and uh, dividing the beat into four equal sections. This is written as 1 e + a.

1 e + a 2 e + a   1 e + a 2 e + a

1. Write the counts below the following notes.

1 e + a

2. Add bar lines to the following measures.

3. Add time signatures to these rhythms.

Triplets

A triplet is a group of three notes played in the time of one note of the next large value.

Not all groups of three notes are triplets. A triplet always has the number 3 over or under the notes.

An eighth note triplet fills the time of one quarter note.

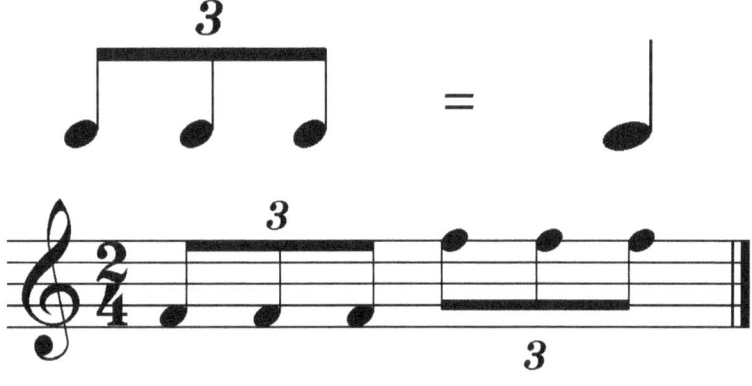

1. Add bar lines to the following rhythms.

Dotted Eighth Notes

A dot after a note increases its value by half. The example below shows a dotted half note worth 3 beats and a dotted quarter worth 1 ½ beats.

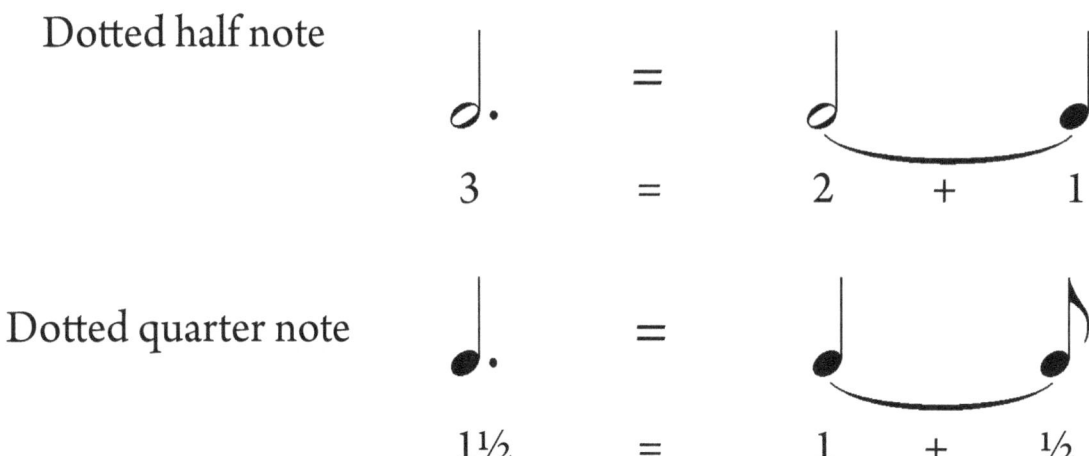

The example below contains a dotted eighth note. An eighth note is worth ½ of a beat. The dot is equal to a sixteenth note. A sixteenth note is worth ¼ of a beat. The dotted eighth is equal to ¾ of a beat.

Think of a dotted eighth note like a pie. The whole pie is 1 beat. An eighth note is ½ of the pie and a sixteenth note is ¼ of the pie. A dotted eighth (½ + ¼) is ¾ of the pie, or ¾ of a beat.

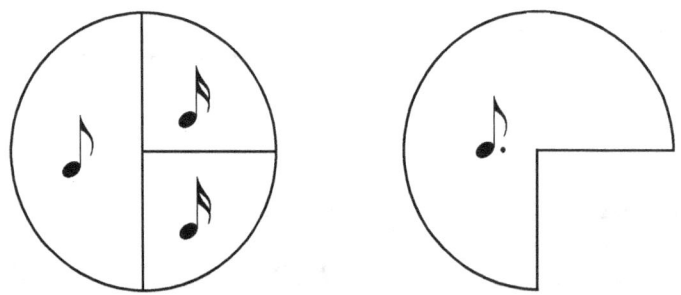

The dotted eighth note is often seen in combination with a sixteenth note. The dotted eighth is connected by a beam to a sixteenth note. This creates one complete beat and is a common rhythmic figure.

1. Add bar lines to the following rhythms.

The Upbeat or Anacrusis

The first beat of a measure is the strongest and is called the downbeat. Some pieces begin on an unaccented or less strong beat. This is called an upbeat, pick-up, or anacrusis.

When a melody begins on an upbeat, both the first and last measure will be incomplete. The melody below begins on an upbeat. It begins on beat 3, a weak beat. The first note of this melody is a quarter note upbeat. The first and last measures of this melody are incomplete. The third beat which is missing from the last measure is equal to the upbeat in the first measure. These two incomplete measures add up to one complete measure. No rests are needed with incomplete measures.

For He's a Jolly Good Fellow
Traditional

Rests

Music is made up of a combination of notes and rests. Rests indicate durations of silence. There is a saying that "notes are silver, rests are golden." Rests play a very important role in making music.

Review the following rests and their values in quarter time.

whole rest	𝄻	= 4 beats
half rest	𝄼	= 2 beats
quarter rest	𝄽	= 1 beat
eighth rest	𝄾	= ½ beat
sixteenth rest	𝄿	= ¼ beat

A whole rest is used to indicate one complete measure of silence no matter what time signature is used.

1. Write one rest which is equal to the value of these groups of rests.

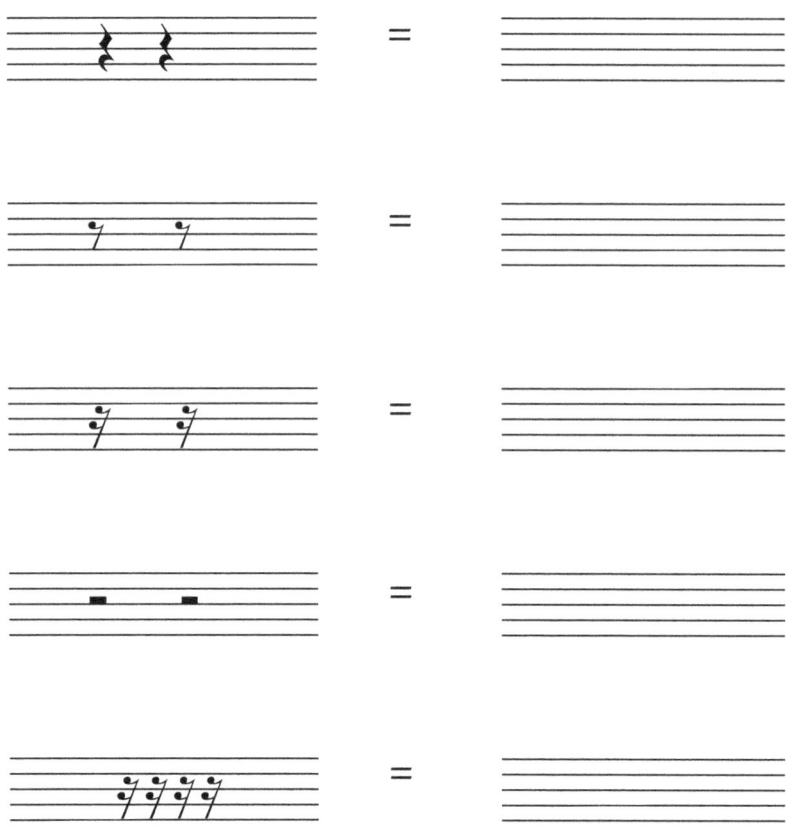

2. Add one rest to complete each measure.

Italian Terms Referring to Tempo

Slow	*largo*	very slow and broad
	larghetto	not as slow as largo
	lento	slow
	adagio	slow (slower than andante, but not as slow as largo)
Medium	*andante*	moderately slow; walking pace
	andantino	a little faster than andante
	moderato	at moderate tempo
Fast	*allegretto*	fairly fast (a little slower than allegro)
	allegro	fast
	presto	very fast
	prestissimo	as fast as possible
	vivace	lively; brisk

Review Quiz 2

1. Write the following key signatures.

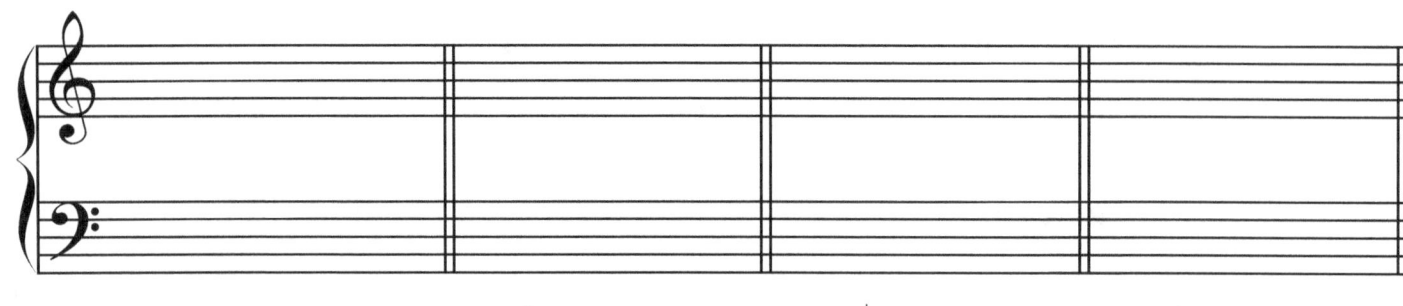

    F major   D major   B♭ major   G major

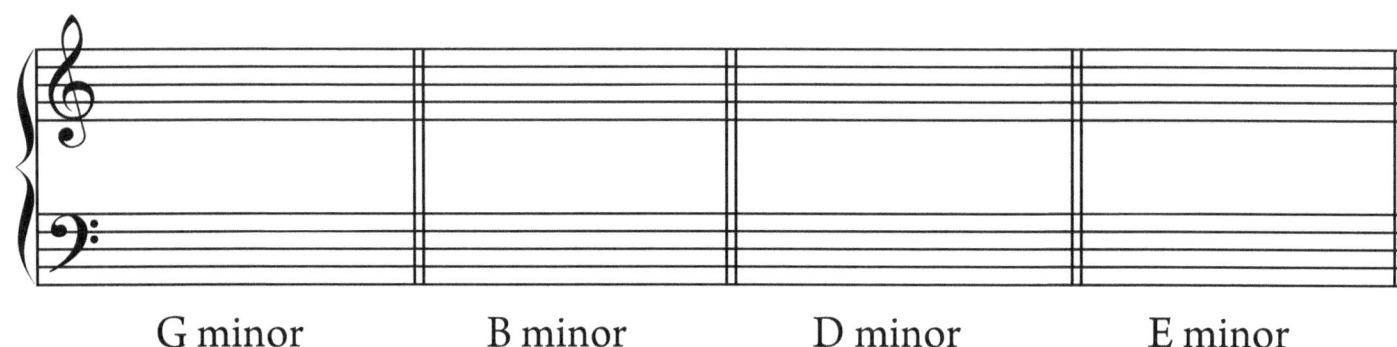

    G minor   B minor   D minor   E minor

2. Write the following scales ascending and descending using key signatures. Mark the leading tones with LT.

D major

A melodic minor

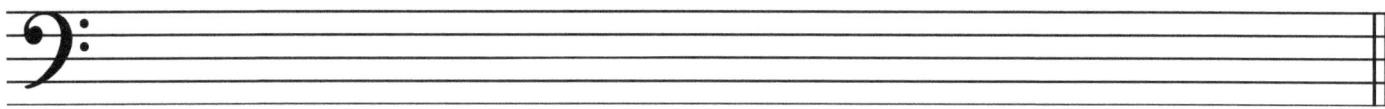

G harmonic minor

3. Mark the following as chromatic half steps (C), diatonic half steps (D), or whole steps (W).

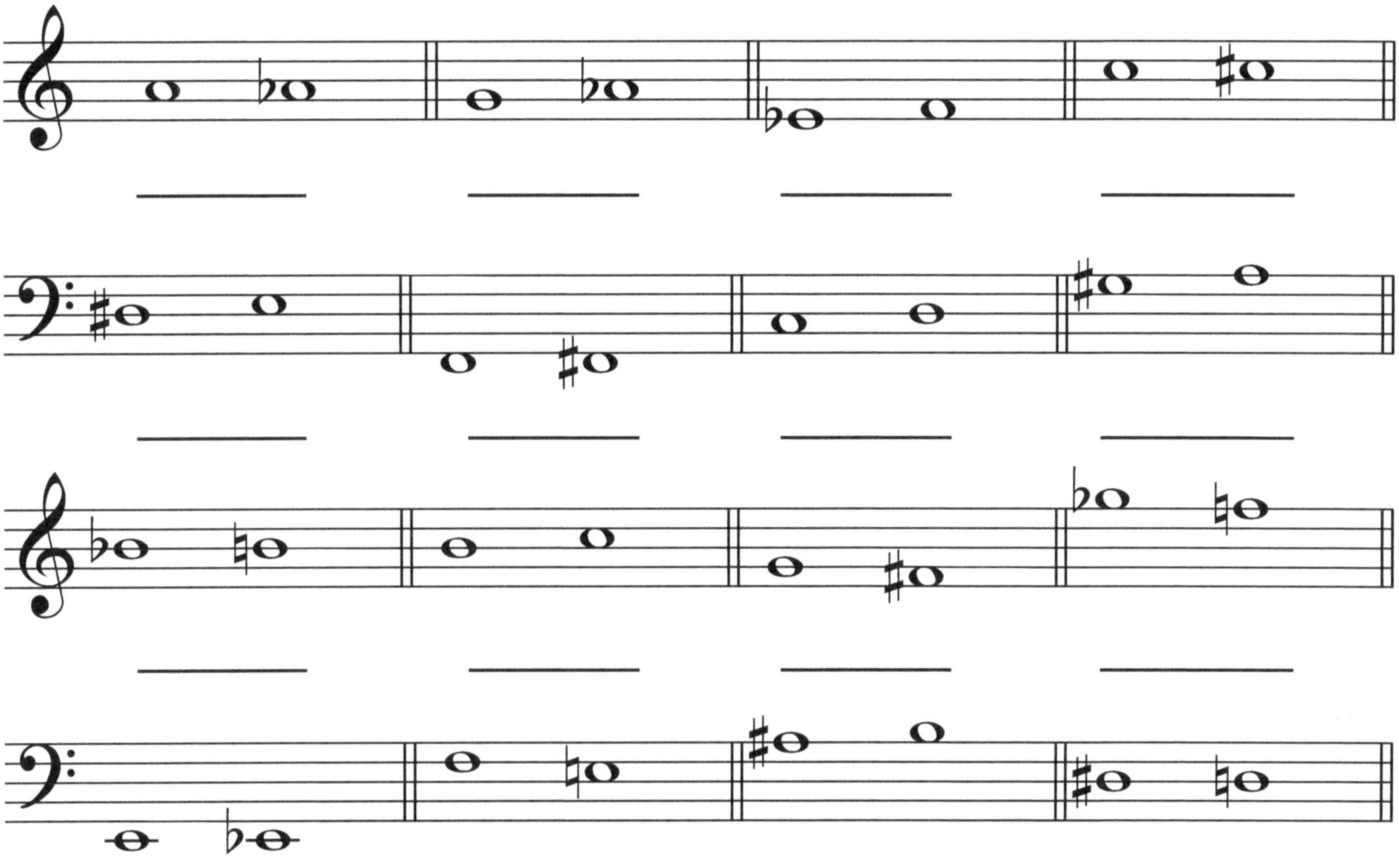

4. Write these intervals above the given notes.

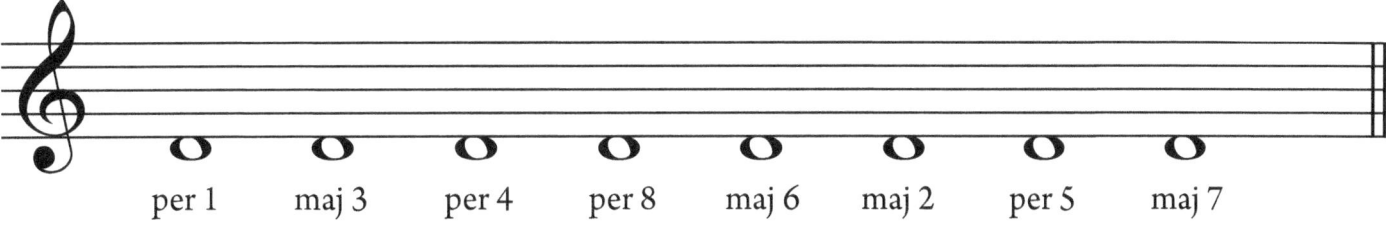

5. Add bar lines to the following examples.

6. Draw lines matching the following Italian terms with their definitions.

presto	a slow tempo, not as slow as largo
adagio	fast
largo	return to the original tempo
allegro	in a singing style
dolce	very fast
mano sinistra m.s	right hand
cantabile	as fast as possible
vivace	sweet, gentle
prestissimo	lively, brisk
mano destra m.d.	very slow
a tempo	left hand

The Percussion Section

All instruments that are played by being hit with something are percussion instruments. There are many percussion instruments. Examples of these are:

timpani
bass drum
snare drum
gong
triangle
tambourine
castanets
and many more.

cymbals
chimes
xylophone
marimba
piano
celesta,
maracas

Triads

A chord is a group of notes that are played together.
A triad is a chord that has three notes.

Lets look at a triad that is built on the first note of the C major scale.

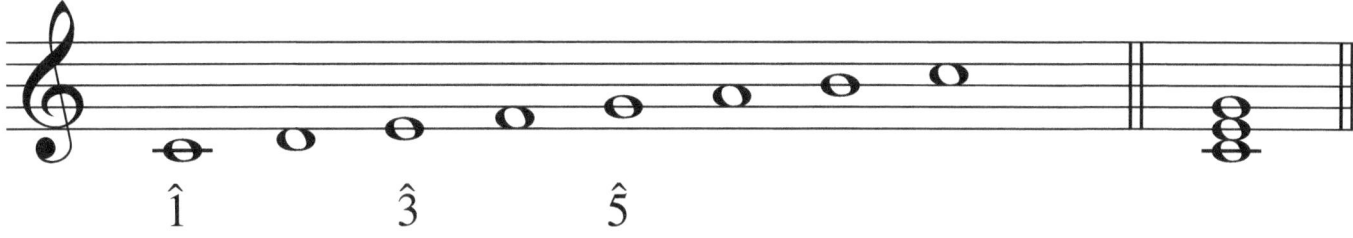

The three notes of a triad have names:

- The bottom note is the **root**.
- The middle note is called the **third**. This note is a major 3rd above the root.
- The top note is called the **fifth**. This note is a perfect 5th above the root.

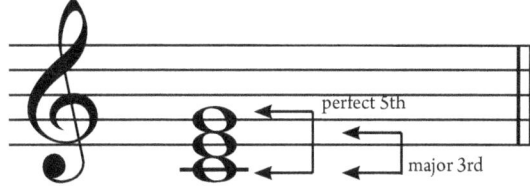

In other words, a major triad is made up of a major 3rd and a perfect 5th.
The first note of the scale is called the **tonic**.
The triad built on the tonic of a major scale is called the tonic major triad.

Chord Symbols

We can give triads chord symbols. Chord symbols are used to identify and label chords.

The root/quality chord symbol is placed on top of the triad and for the C major triad below, is a capital C. This means it is a C major triad. A capital or uppercase letter always refers to a major triad. The root/quality chord symbol G would mean a G major triad.

We can place a chord symbol under the triad as well. This is called a functional chord symbol. Functional chord symbols use Roman numerals to identify chords.

Since this is the triad built on the tonic, or scale degree $\hat{1}$ of C major, it gets the Roman numeral uppercase **I** as its functional chord symbol. This means it is the triad built on the first scale degree, or tonic, and uppercase means it is a major triad, consisting of a major 3rd and perfect 5th above the root.

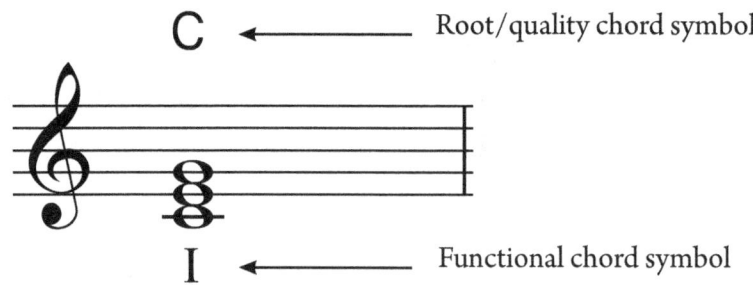

1. Write the following scales using accidentals. Label the first, third, and fifth notes of the scale ($\hat{1}$, $\hat{3}$, $\hat{5}$). Write the tonic major triad for each. Add the root/quality and functional chord symbols for each chord.

2. Write the root/quality and functional chord symbols for the following major tonic triads.

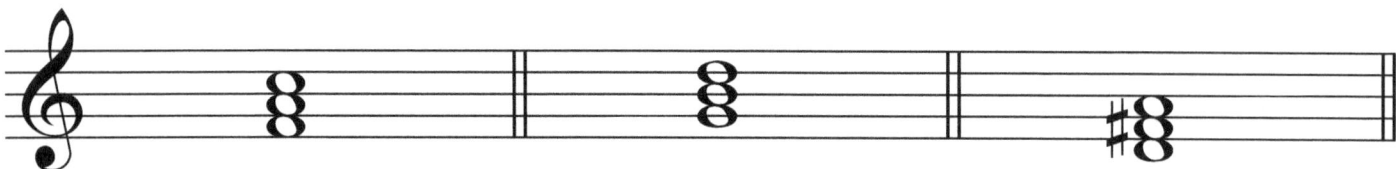

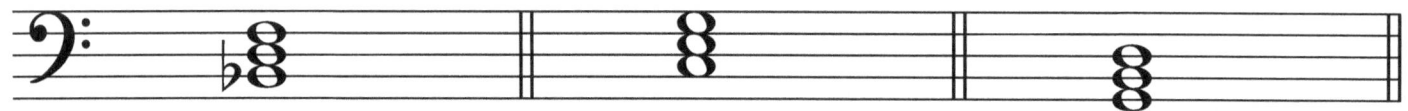

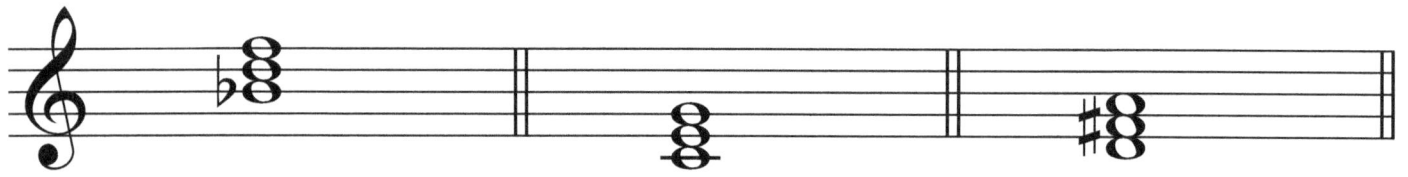

3. Write the following triads using accidentals. Add the root/quality chord symbol above each.

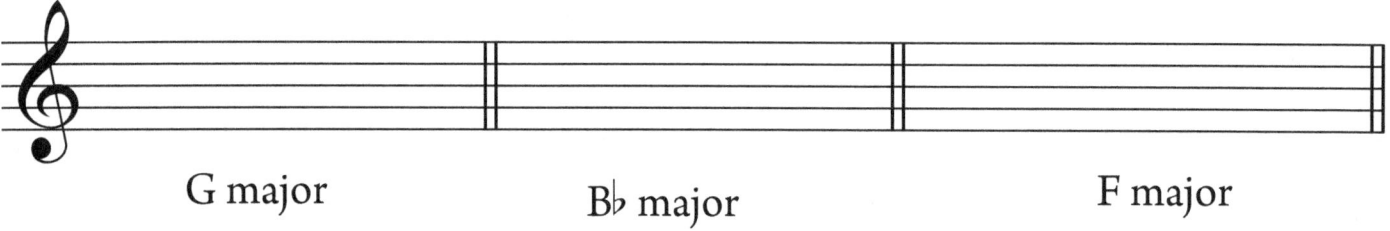

G major   B♭ major   F major

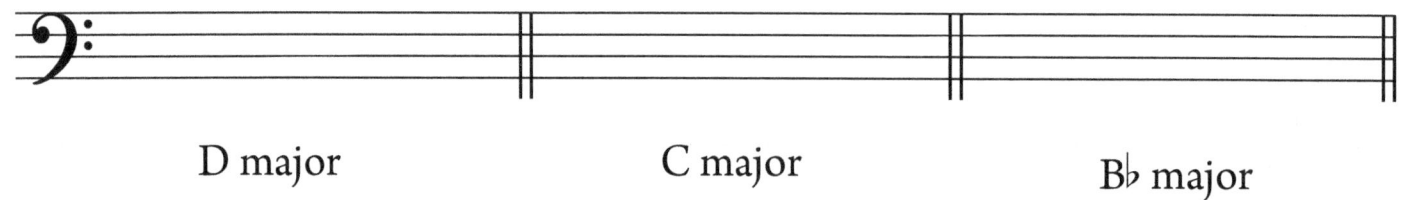

D major   C major   B♭ major

Broken Triads

The notes of a triad may be played solid (together). Another name for solid is blocked. Or they may be played broken which is playing the notes one after the other.

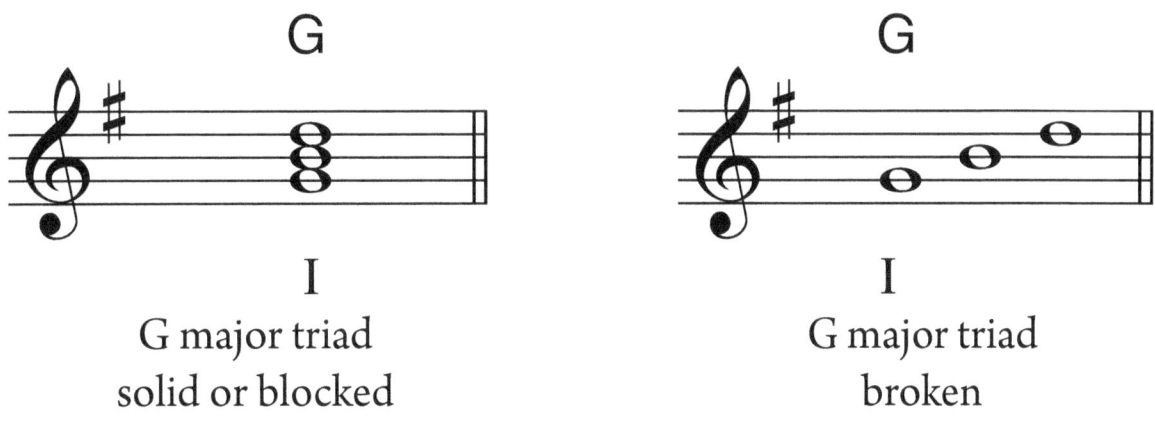

1. Write the following broken triads using key signatures. Add the root/quality and functional chord symbols.

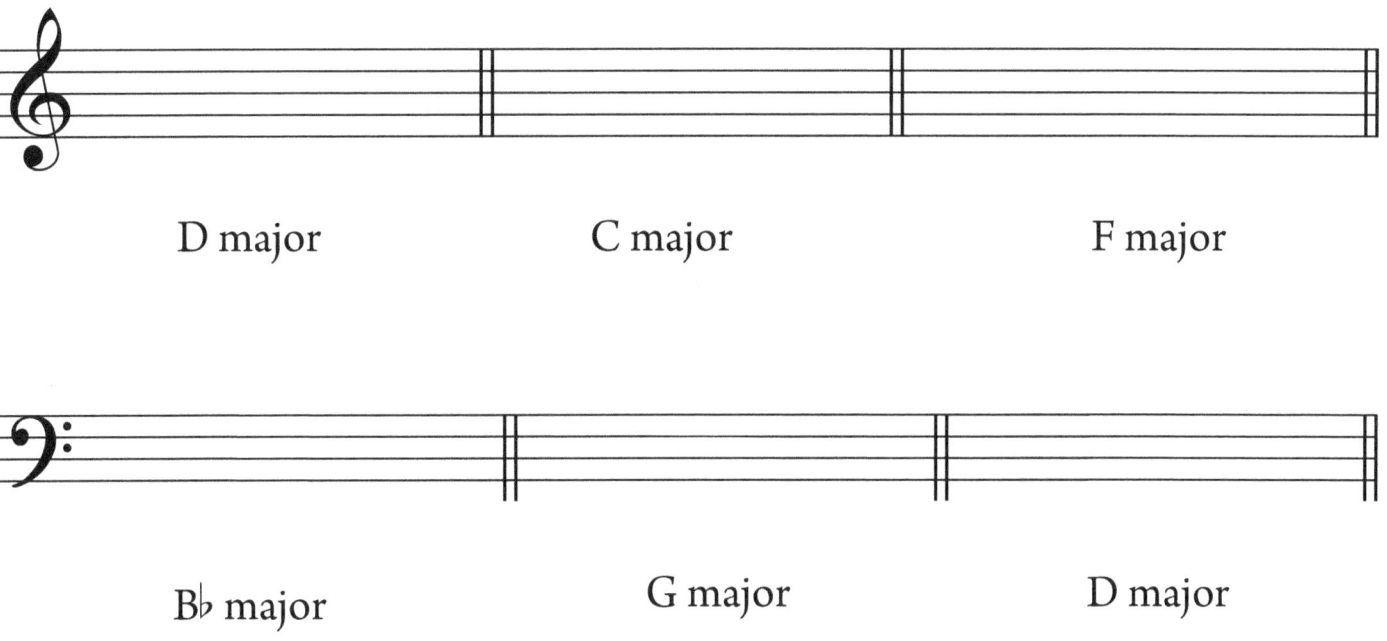

The Dominant Triad

A triad may also be built on the dominant. This is called the dominant triad. The dominant triad is built by stacking thirds on scale degree $\hat{5}$ of any major scale.

When you stack thirds on the 5th note of the C major scale you get the G major triad (G B D). For this triad, G is the root, B is the 3rd and D is the 5th.

This is a G major triad so the root/quality chord symbol is a capital G. The functional chord symbol is the uppercase Roman numeral **V**. This means that it is a major triad built on scale degree $\hat{5}$.

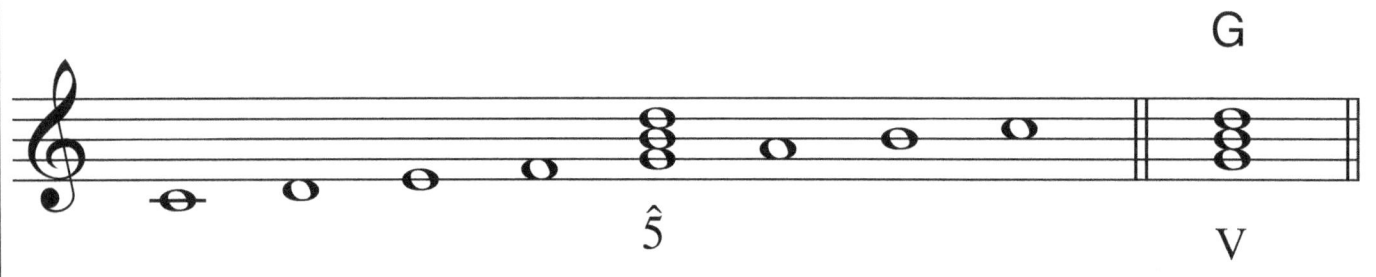

1. Write the following major scales ascending using accidentals. Write the dominant triad on scale degree $\hat{5}$. Re-write the triad in the second bar with the root/quality and functional chord symbols.

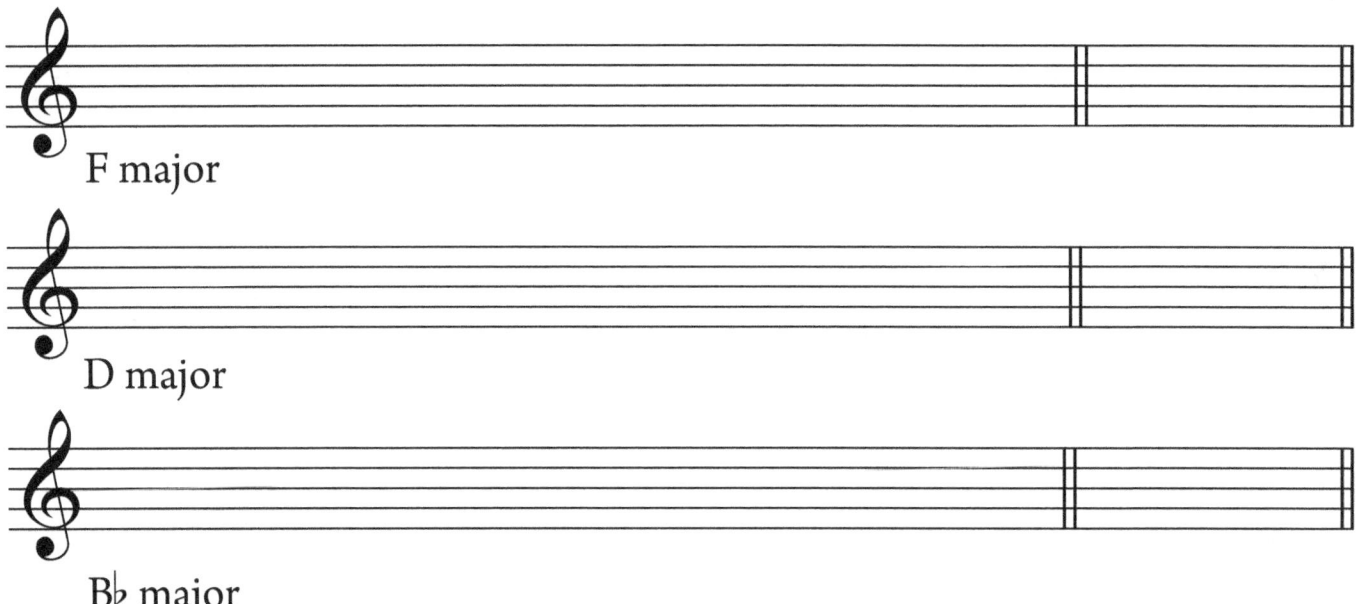

F major

D major

B♭ major

2. Using key signatures write dominant triads in the following keys. Add the root/quality and functional chord symbols for each.

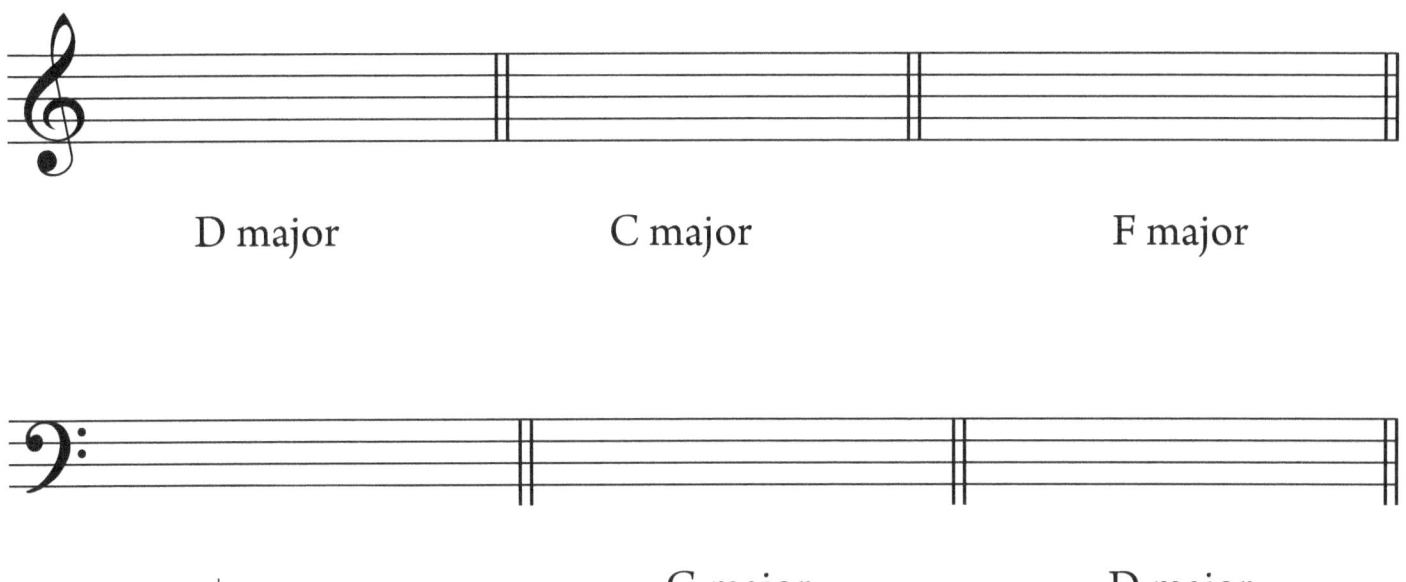

3. Add root/quality and functional chord symbols to the following dominant triads.

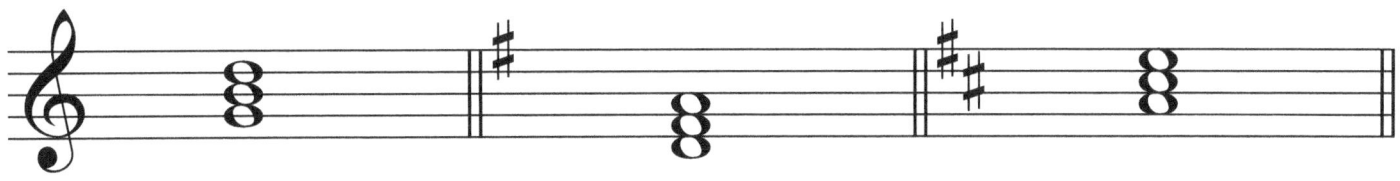

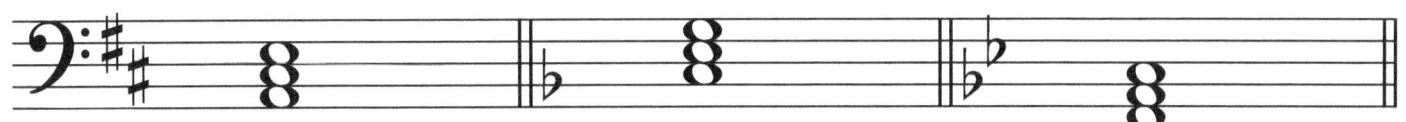

WORD SCRAMBLE

Unscramble the words to find Italian musical terms.

lelrgetota ___ ___ ___ ___ ___ ___ (_) ___

ntalibcae ___ ___ ___ ___ ___ ___ ___

garol ___ ___ ___ ___ ___

leglroa ___ ___ (_) ___ ___ ___

odreatmo (_) ___ ___ ___ ___ ___ ___ ___

stismoespri (_) ___ ___ ___ ___ ___ ___ ___ ___ ___

celdo ___ ___ ___ ___ ___

avceiv ___ ___ ___ ___ ___ ___

tandena ___ ___ ___ ___ ___ ___ ___

gadioa ___ ___ ___ ___ ___ (_)

Copy the circled letters to reveal the hidden word:

___ ___ ___ ___ ___ ___

63

Review Quiz 3

1. Name these notes.

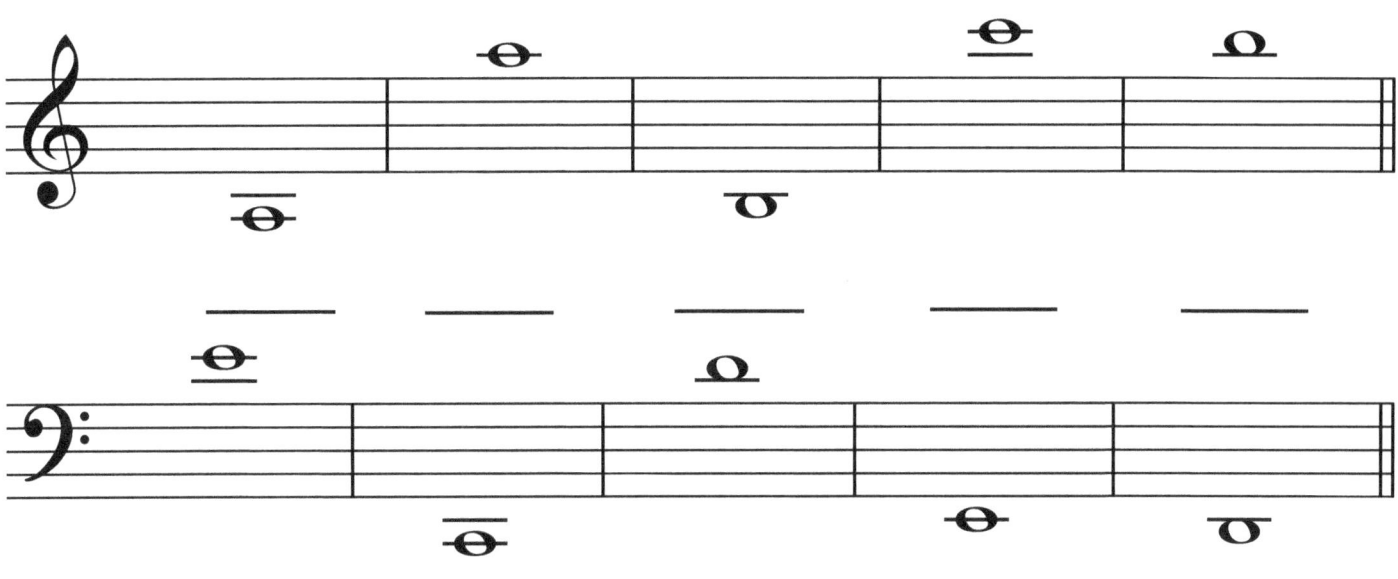

2. Write the following scales ascending and descending using key signatures. Label the subtonic notes (ST).

B natural minor

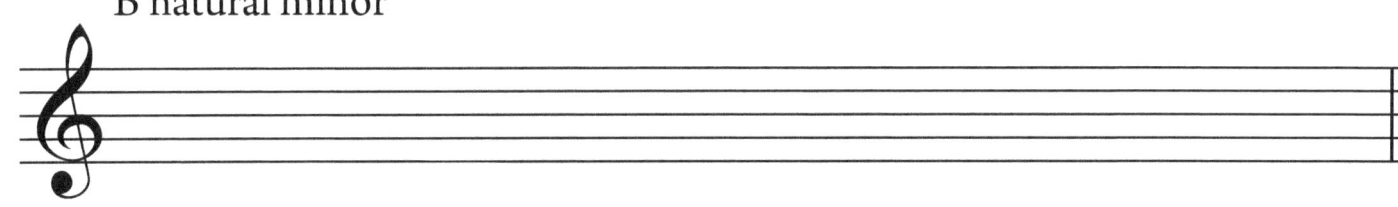

D melodic minor

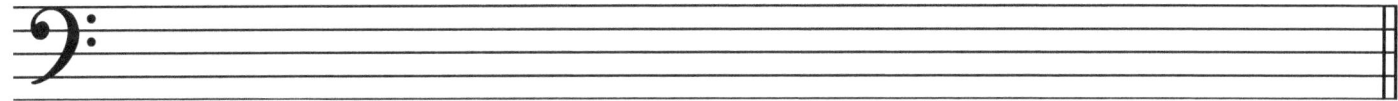

G harmonic minor

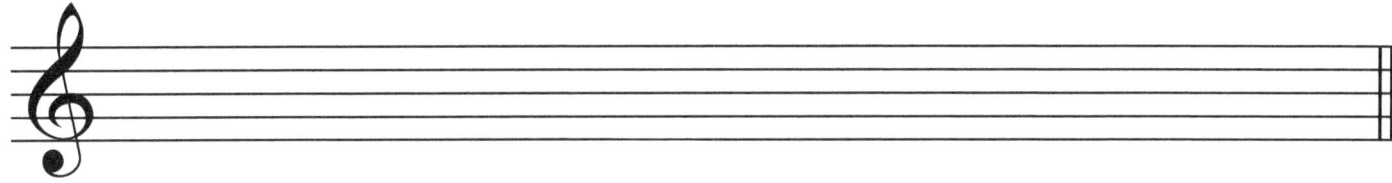

3. Name the following intervals.

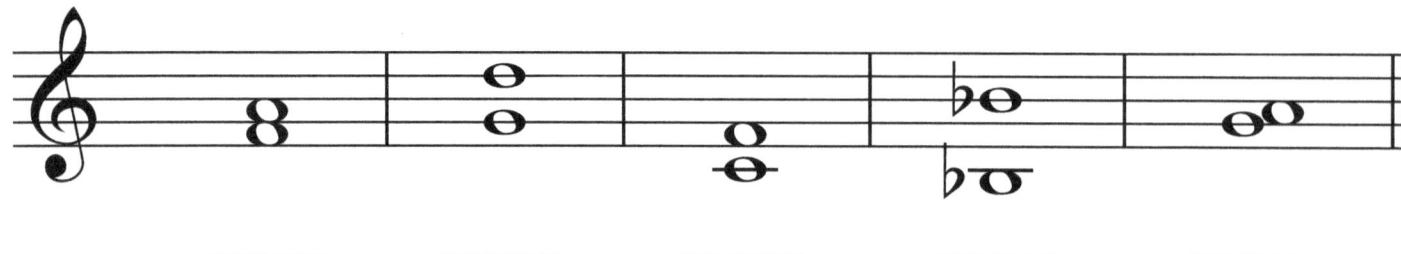

4. Write chromatic half steps above the following notes.

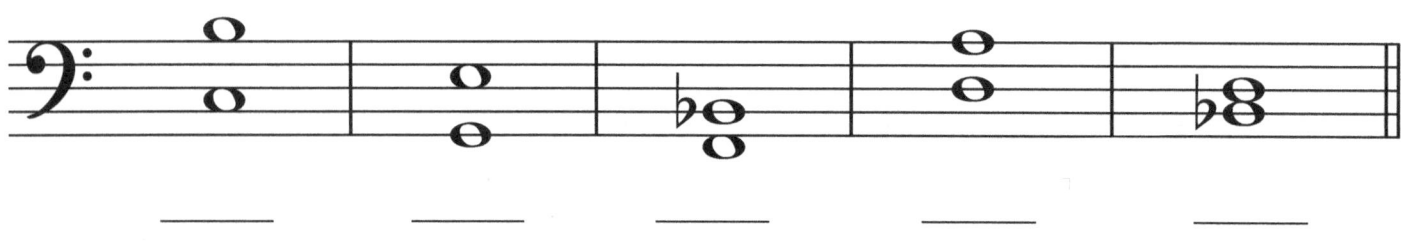

5. Write diatonic half steps below the following notes.

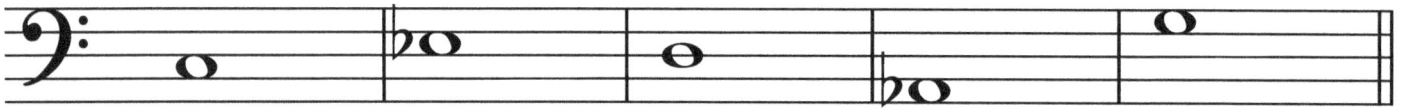

6. Write whole steps above the following notes.

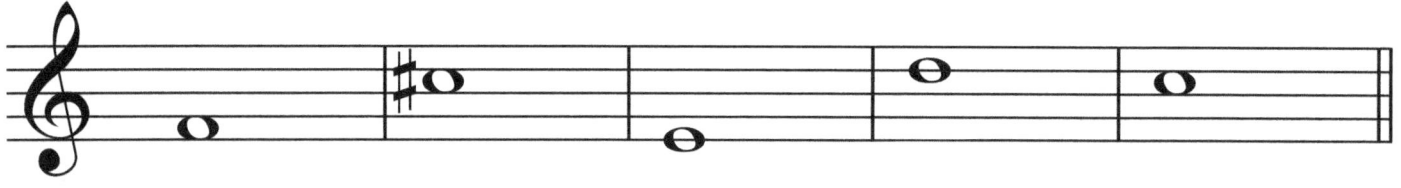

7. Add time signatures to the following rhythms.

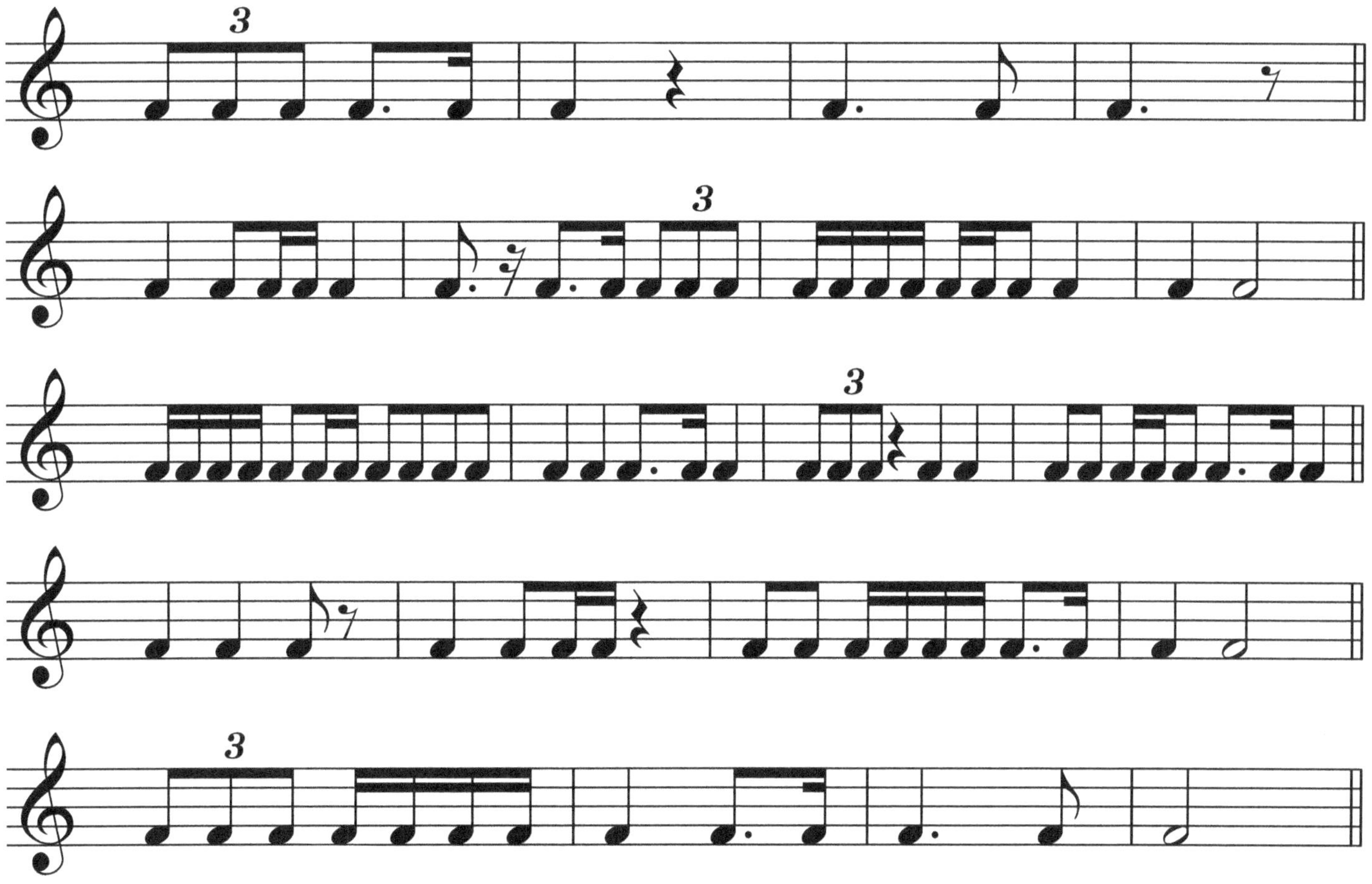

20

8. Add one rest to complete each measure.

15

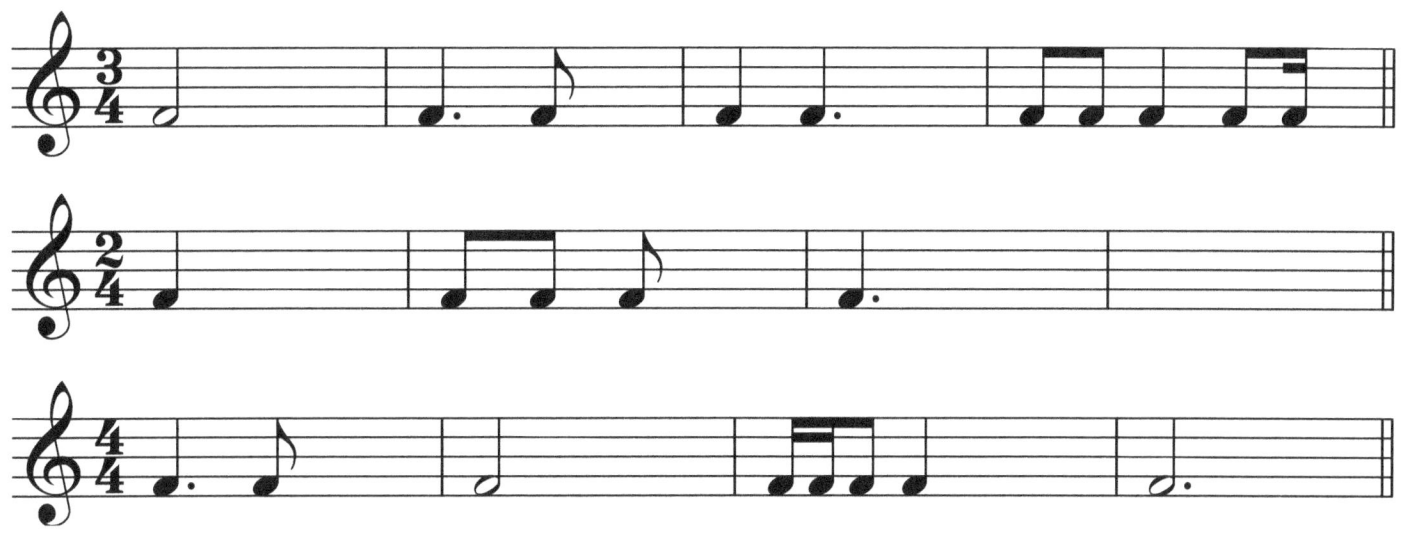

9. Using key signatures, write the following triads according to the chord symbols.

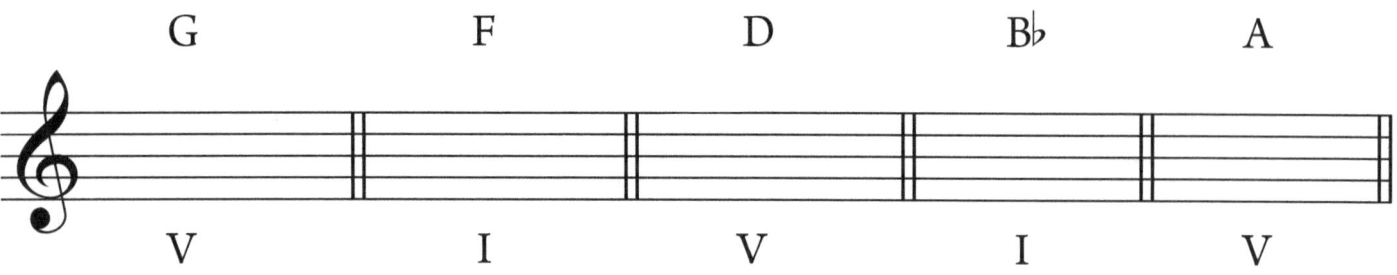

| G | F | D | B♭ | A |
| V | I | V | I | V |

___
5

10. Define the following Italian terms.

cantabile _____

presto _____

allegretto _____

mano sinistra _____

largo _____

dolce _____

adagio _____

prestissimo _____

allegro _____

lento _____

Music Analysis

1. Analyze the music by answering the questions below.

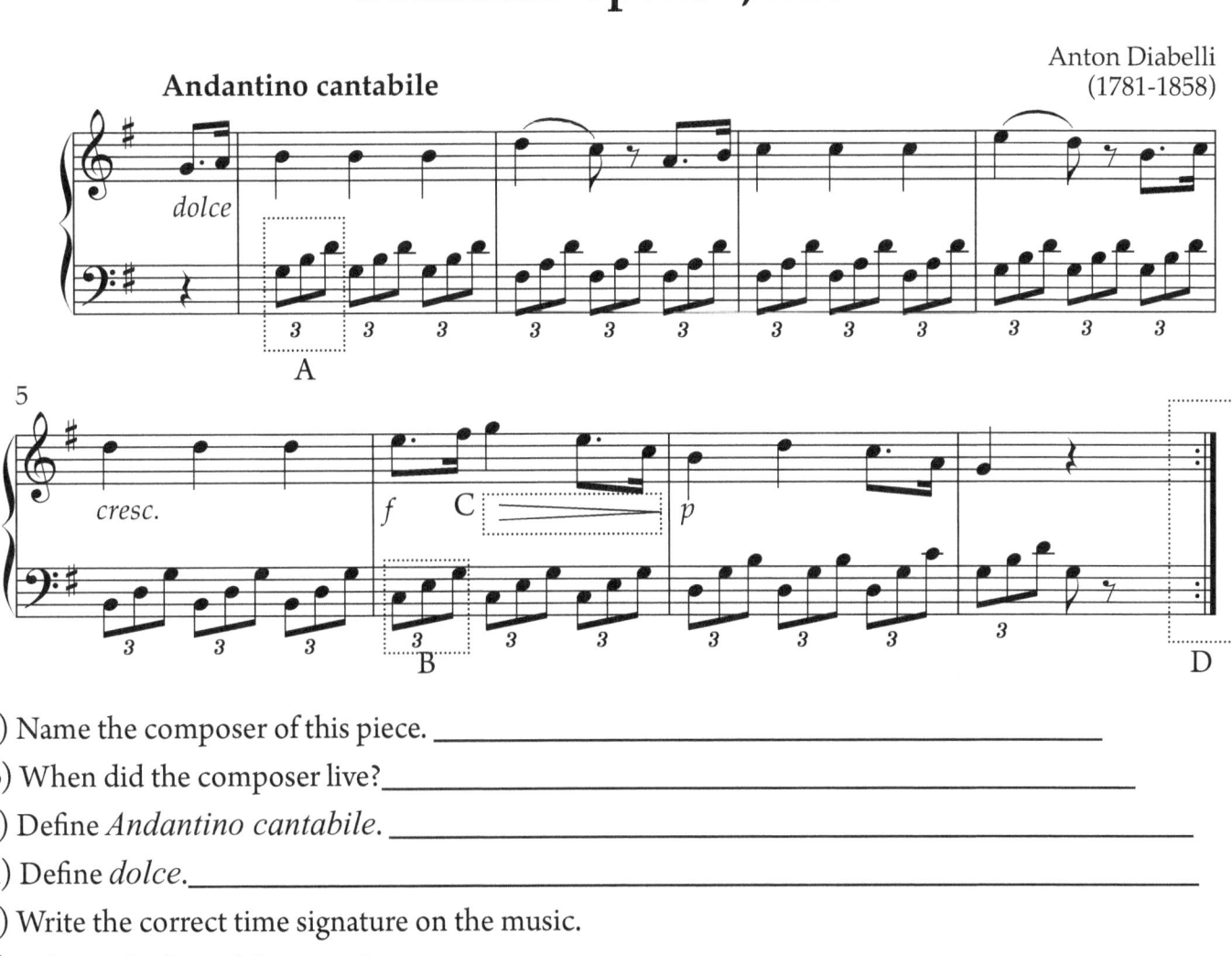

(a) Name the composer of this piece. _____

(b) When did the composer live? _____

(c) Define *Andantino cantabile*. _____

(d) Define *dolce*. _____

(e) Write the correct time signature on the music.

(f) What is the key of this piece? _____

(g) How many measures are in this piece? _____

(h) Name the broken triad at letter A. _____

(i) Name the broken triad at letter B. _____

(j) Explain the sign at letter C. _____

(k) Explain the sign at letter D. _____

(l) Define *cresc.* _____

(m) What is the highest note in this piece? _____

(n) What is the lowest note in this piece? _____

(o) What beat does this piece begin on? _____

(p) What is this incomplete beat called? _____

2. Analyze the music by answering the questions below.

Menuetto

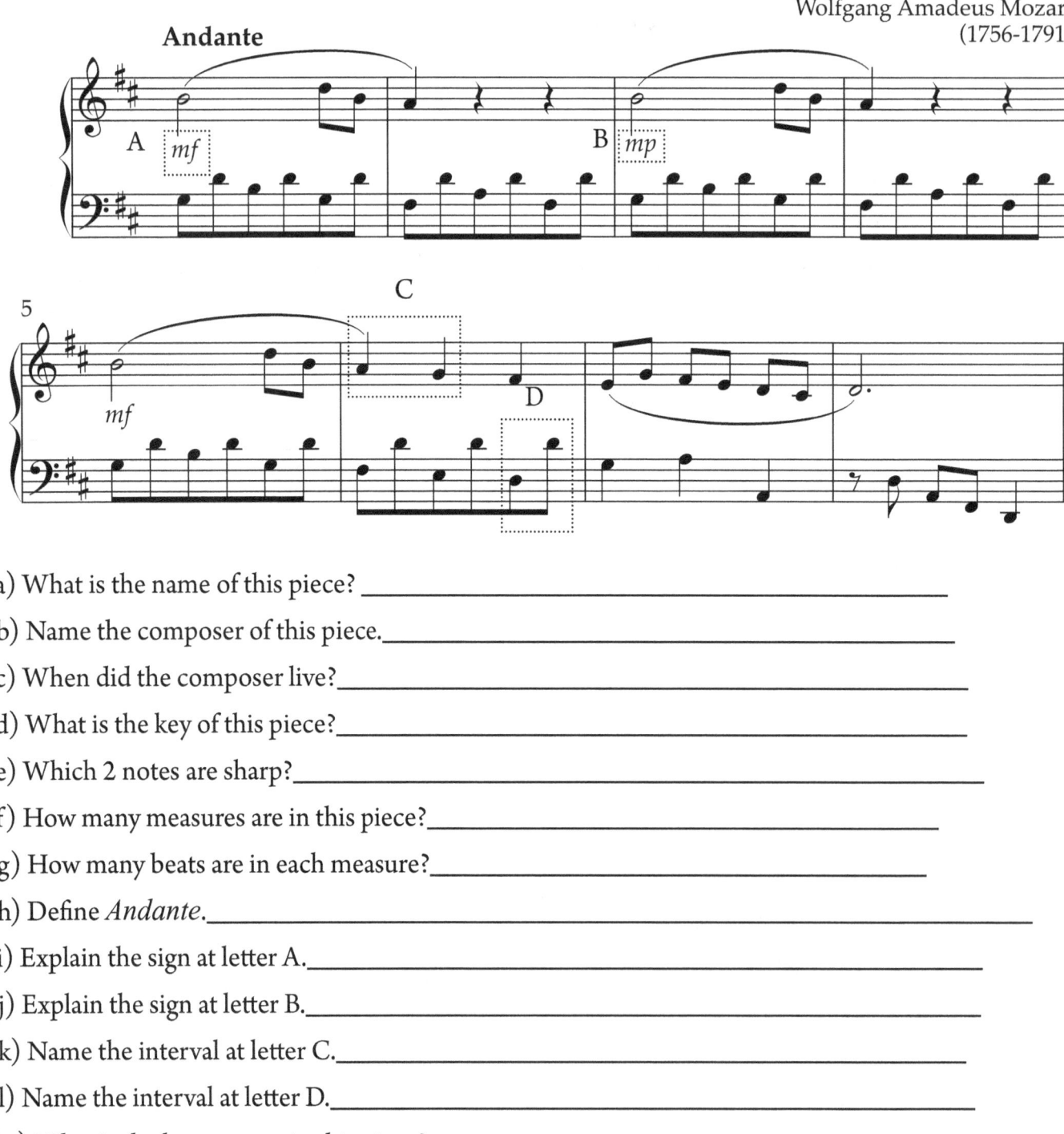

(a) What is the name of this piece? _____

(b) Name the composer of this piece. _____

(c) When did the composer live? _____

(d) What is the key of this piece? _____

(e) Which 2 notes are sharp? _____

(f) How many measures are in this piece? _____

(g) How many beats are in each measure? _____

(h) Define *Andante*. _____

(i) Explain the sign at letter A. _____

(j) Explain the sign at letter B. _____

(k) Name the interval at letter C. _____

(l) Name the interval at letter D. _____

(m) What is the lowest note in this piece? _____

(n) Add the time signature directly on the score.

Congratulations! You have completed Elementary Music Theory Book 3! You are ready for Essential Music Theory Book 4!

Certificate of Achievement

CONGRATULATIONS TO

_____

You have completed

ELEMENTARY MUSIC THEORY BOOK 3

You are now ready for Essential Music Theory Book 4

3

Teacher_____

Date_____

www.ingramcontent.com/pod-product-compliance
Lightning Source LLC
Chambersburg PA
CBHW081711100526
44590CB00022B/3736